Para Pro

Supporting the Instructional Process

Instructional Assistants (IA)

Teacher Aides (TA)

Classroom Support Staff

Duty Supervisors

Paraprofessionals

Educational Assistants (EA)

Paraeducators

Randy Sprick

Mickey Garrison

Lisa Howard

10   09   08   07   8   7   6

ISBN 1-599909-000-7 (previously ISBN 1-57035-309-3)

Printed in the United States of America

Published and Distributed by:

Pacific
Northwest
Publishing

2451 Willamette St • Eugene, OR 97405
(866) 542-1490 • (541) 345-1490
www.pacificnwpublish.com

Dedication

To my mom, Marjean Sprick, who encouraged and supported me when I became a paraeducator, when I became a teacher, and in everything else I have tried. R.S.

To the "Randys" in my life—Randy Sprick for his friendship, guidance, and vision; and Randy Garrison for his love, support, and commitment to our relationship. M.G.

ACKNOWLEDGEMENTS

We would like to express our admiration and appreciation for paraeducators and the vitally important contributions they make in schools. In particular we want to acknowledge the following paraeducators for their skill and their commitment to children:

- Ginnie Olson
- Martha Sohlich
- Penny West
- All the instructional assistants at Sunnyslope Intermediate School

In addition, we would like to thank:

- Fern Healy, Marilyn Sprick, Ray Beck, Steve Kukic, Deb Hanson, and Bertha Caldwell for their content suggestions and feedback;
- Chuck Marier for his great illustrations;
- Katherine Getta for her creative design and layout; and
- Cheryl Mikkola for her careful copyediting.

Table of Contents

Introduction

The prefix para- is defined as "at the side of, beside, alongside of." A paraeducator, therefore, is a person who works alongside of the teachers, specialists, and administrators in a school. Please note that although in this book we use the term "paraeducator" to describe someone who fills this role, individuals in these positions may also go by the title of teacher assistant, assistant teacher, paraprofessional, instructional assistant, or educational assistant, among others. Regardless of your title, if you work at the side of the professional staff in your school, the work you do is vitally important. You can and should get a great deal of satisfaction in knowing that you are helping your school's students and staff.

The job of a paraeducator, however, is neither simple nor easy. The purpose of this book is to provide information that will help you function more effectively and successfully as a paraeducator. We recognize that working as a paraeducator can at times seem overwhelming. That is why, throughout the book, we have incorporated the following five-point star to help you stay focused on the most important traits of effective paraeducators: Professional, Planful, Positive, Persistent, Patient.

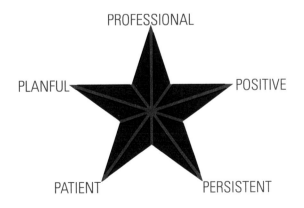

PROFESSIONAL

PLANFUL

POSITIVE

PATIENT

PERSISTENT

If you keep these five traits in mind as you attend to your job responsibilities, you will be successful. As new ideas and suggestions are introduced in the book, you will find the star with one or more of its points highlighted to indicate which trait(s) are being emphasized.

This book has seven chapters, representing major areas of information or work responsibilities that are important to a paraeducator. Within each chapter you will find a series of three to seven tasks designed to help you understand or improve in that area. Each task starts with an introduction that provides a brief overview and highlights which of the star points to keep in mind as you read the task. Each task then has a "How To Do It" section that offers specific information, suggestions, and strategies that will enable you to implement the task.

For example, Chapter 5, entitled "Working with Small Groups," addresses how a paraeducator can effectively support instruction when the job assignment involves working with a small group of students. Task 5 of that chapter is: Use effective instructional techniques. The introduction to this task presents the star with the Persistent point highlighted. That's because the really important message about working with a small group is to persistently present (and re-present as necessary) the information to the students until they demonstrate mastery of it.

To help clarify the information and ideas in this book, we have added one additional feature. Please meet the "Para-Pros" and "Para-Cons."

You will find these characters throughout the book. The Para-Cons will show examples of what NOT to do. The Para-Pros, on the other hand, will model the right way to do things. Because the Para-Pros constantly strive to be professional, planful, positive, patient, and persistent, they will always be wearing a star.

GETTING THE MOST FROM THIS BOOK

Being planful is one of the five traits of a star paraeducator, and part of being planful is being reflective about yourself and what you do. Thus, in your work as a paraeducator, you should be constantly asking yourself questions like, What is going well? What is not going well? What can I do differently to improve the things that are not going well? In the same way, we strongly suggest that as you read through this book, you use the information to evaluate how you are currently doing your job and what you might do to improve.

Start by reflecting on the suggestions in the book that seem easy for you—things you already do effectively without having to make a conscious effort. For example, in Chapter 2 (Being Part of the School Team), Task 1 recommends that you demonstrate a positive attitude when interacting with students and staff. Among the "How To Do It" suggestions are to smile frequently and to exhibit a "Can do!" approach to challenges. If you are a positive and friendly person by nature, you might mentally pat yourself on the back as you read these suggestions and remind yourself to keep doing those things that you already do well.

Perhaps more importantly, though, you need to identify and reflect on those suggestions in the book that do not seem as easy for you. For example, in Chapter 4 (Supervising Common Areas), Task 2 discusses the importance of circulating and scanning when you are supervising a setting such as a cafeteria-that is, being planful about how you supervise. As you read this task, honestly evaluate your own behavior in these situations. Ask yourself whether you talk so much with other adults that you do not circulate

to different parts of the cafeteria, for example. If the answer is yes, then you need to make a plan to talk less and circulate more.

Please note that the preceding two examples show how the same personality characteristic that is a strength can also be a weakness. That is, being friendly and positive by nature may make it easy for you to get along with the other adults in the school, but may also contribute to your being less effective when it comes to supervising common areas. As you read through this book, take the time to carefully consider your own practices. If you identify an area of possible weakness or something you think you need to know more about, determine what you need to do to improve. THEN DO IT!

To help you with this self-reflection process, you will find an Activities section at the end of each of the chapters in the book. The first activity in this section will always be a Think About It chart on which you can rate your current knowledge and/or skill level for each of the tasks presented in that chapter (see Figure 0.1). For any task(s) that you give yourself a 2, 3, or 4 rating, we suggest that you put a prompt of some kind in your planning calendar to reread or discuss the task(s) at an appropriate time during the school year. If you do this activity for each chapter, the book can serve as a guide to your ongoing efforts to improve your skills.

Figure 0.1 from **Think About It** *chart for Chapter 1*

	The information was not applicable to my situation.	The information was familiar. I consistently implement the strategies presented.	The information was useful. I should reread this task at least once more this year.	Some of the information was new. I should reread this task within a month.	Much of the information was new. I should discuss it with my supervisor or with other paraeducators.
TASK 1: Remember the "bare essentials."	0	1	2	3	4
TASK 2: Understand the hierarchy of authority in your school	0	1	2	3	4

The second activity will suggest a way to Take Action—that is, to collect information about some aspect(s) of your job performance and, as necessary, make improvements. For example, in Chapter 5 (Working with Small Groups), the Take Action activity describes a system for rating the behavior of students in your small group to determine which aspects of their behavior, if any, need to improve.

The third activity is a set of Discuss It questions/topics to review with other paraeducators. One of the most powerful ways to expand your own knowledge and skill as a paraeducator is to work with your peers. If one or more of the paraeducators in your school is interested, you might try to arrange for regularly scheduled study group meetings (e.g., every other Tuesday after school). Prior to each meeting, all the participants should read the same chapter in the book and implement the Take Action suggestion(s) for that chapter. During the meeting, then, the group can discuss the items for that chapter. Note that the final item for this activity in all of the chapters is, "Have each person share any useful ideas that were gained from working through the Take Action activity for this chapter."

As a paraeducator, you have the opportunity to make a difference. You help provide the education that can change students' lives for the better. It is our hope that this book will help you in this noble and important role.

CHAPTER 1

Understanding the Basics

Your job as a paraeducator is important. The work can be fun, and there is no question that you can help many people. It also can be a difficult and demanding job. You may be given a lot of responsibility (e.g., making sure students are safe on the school playground), possibly without a lot of information and often without a lot of authority. You are likely to have several "bosses," including the school principal and various teachers, some of whom may not always communicate effectively with you or with each other. Your schedule may change frequently and without warning. We believe you can and will be more successful and satisfied as a paraeducator if you understand and attend to some basic ideas.

This chapter begins with Task 1—a one-page list of "bare essentials" which are just that-minimum considerations to help the beginning paraeducator get through the first couple of weeks on the job. (This task, which is geared to someone who has never worked in a school before, should be reviewed before you start your job as a paraeducator. Experienced paraeducators may wish to skim or even skip the task.)

Tasks 2, 3, and 4 elaborate on some basics of being a successful paraeducator: respecting the hierarchy of authority in your school; presenting yourself in a professional manner; and treating everyone in your school with dignity and respect. The chapter ends with Task 5, a brief introduction to some basic legal issues you should be aware of when working in a school.

The specific tasks in Chapter 1 are:

1. Remember the "bare essentials."

2. Understand the hierarchy of authority in your school.

3. Present yourself in a professional manner.

4. Treat everyone in the school with dignity and respect.

5. Be aware of some basic school-based legal issues.

As you read this chapter, notice that the "Professional" point on the five-point star has been highlighted for most of the tasks. That is because being a successful paraeducator requires a professional approach to the job.

Also, as you read through the chapter remember to watch for the Para-Pro and Para-Con characters. They will give you additional information as well as worthwhile tips and hints.

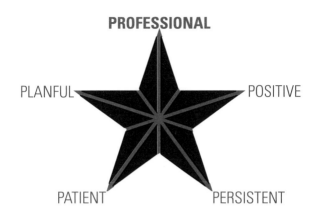

PROFESSIONAL

PLANFUL   POSITIVE

PATIENT   PERSISTENT

TASK 1:

Remember the "bare essentials."

NOTE: This task is geared to the individual who is just getting started as a paraeducator. Experienced paraeducators may wish to skim this task or even skip it completely.

Your first couple of weeks as a paraeducator may seem overwhelming as you learn about your school, your job, and the specific responsibilities you will be expected to carry out. The following "bare essentials" can help you succeed at your job, especially during the first few days. Because they represent fundamental considerations, you will find that these ideas are elaborated on in this chapter and throughout the remainder of the book. For now, however, we simply want to remind you to remember these "bare essentials."

HOW TO DO IT:

• Follow directions.

Do whatever you are asked to do to the best of your ability.

• Ask questions.

Whenever you are not sure how to follow a particular direction, ask. There is no such thing as a stupid question. The school personnel with whom you work would rather you ask a question than pretend to know what you're supposed to be doing when you don't. Don't worry if for the first several days (or even weeks) you frequently find yourself saying, "Could you explain again how you want me to do that?"

• Be flexible and pleasant.

One of the most important characteristics of a successful paraeducator is flexibility. You may not only be asked to adapt to a variety of expectations from different supervisors, but also to do a variety of jobs, all of which may change from day to day. You need to be prepared to handle that variety and those changes—with a smile. A good attitude is critical. Most supervisors will not expect you to know things you have not been taught; however, they will look for an attitude that communicates you're ready and willing to do whatever needs to be done.

- **Avoid disastrous mistakes.**

Notice we did not say, "Don't make mistakes." No one expects you to be perfect, and you probably will make mistakes in your first several weeks. There are, however, a few mistakes that can be disastrous—mistakes that could even cost you your job. These may seem obvious, but:

—*Never hit, grab, or otherwise try to physically move a child.*

—*Never use profanity.*

—*Never breach confidentiality.*

—*Avoid arguments with students or staff.*

—*Avoid being alone, behind closed doors, with only one student.*

- **Have fun!**

If you keep your focus positive and make an effort to enjoy your interactions with students and staff, you will find that being a paraeducator can be rewarding indeed.

ParaPro responds to instructions from immediate supervisors with a positive, "Can do" kind of attitude.

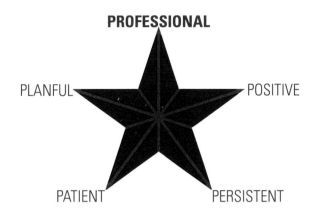

PROFESSIONAL

PLANFUL   POSITIVE

PATIENT   PERSISTENT

TASK 2:

Understand the hierarchy of authority in your school.

For schools to function well, everyone needs to work together. And schools, like most organizations, have a hierarchy of authority to facilitate cooperation. That is, some people in a school have more authority (power) than others. Individuals higher in the hierarchy (i.e., with more authority) are generally responsible for making decisions and for answering questions that may arise. Those lower in the hierarchy (i.e., with less authority) are basically responsible for doing what is asked of them and for asking questions when they are not clear about what that is. We have highlighted the "Professional" point of the star because a professional approach to your job means that you understand the hierarchy of authority in your school and your role in that hierarchy.

As a paraeducator, you are basically responsible for doing what is asked of you by the school's "professional" staff—administrators, teachers, and specialists. In fact, you are likely to find many staff members wanting your time and help, and occasionally you may feel confused

and somewhat frustrated about who to listen to and what to do next. The purpose of this task is to offer suggestions on how to function appropriately and effectively within the basic hierarchy of your school.

HOW TO DO IT:

- **Understand the various levels of supervisors that you may have.**

In most cases, the building principal is the highest level of authority in a school (although she may be under the authority of the Board of Education, the Superintendent of Schools, etc.), making her your ultimate supervisor. The principal is generally the person responsible for hiring you and renewing your position.

The next level of authority is your primary supervisor. This is the person responsible for your schedule and for supporting you in your various roles and responsibilities. In many schools, the primary supervisor for paraeducators is the special education teacher, Title 1 teacher, or behavior specialist. Your primary supervisor is the person with whom you will discuss issues such as changes in schedule, changes in job responsibilities, and problems or disagreements with other staff or students. Keeping this person informed about all aspects of your job is critical if he or she is going to be able to help you do your best and/or advocate for you should that be necessary.

Finally, you may also have one or more immediate supervisors. An immediate supervisor is the person who has direct authority over you in a particular setting (e.g., the cafeteria, a fourth grade classroom). While you are in that setting, this individual is responsible for giving you directions and answering your questions. Your immediate supervisor may change depending on the setting, but your primary supervisor will remain constant.

Depending on the size of your school and/or district, your ultimate, primary, and/or immediate supervisors may be the same person. In any case, understanding the different levels of supervisor is very important. Throughout this book, we will suggest that you check with your supervisor. In some cases, we may specify "primary" or "immediate," but in many cases we will not. In those cases, you need to determine for yourself the most appropriate person to turn to for the information.

Please note that in addition to your supervisors, there are likely to be others in the school—other administrators, teachers, specialists (e.g., school psychologist, counselor, speech/language therapist, occupational therapist, physical therapist, social worker)—with more authority than you. There may even be other paraeducators who, due to experience and seniority, have more authority than you. Although these people may not be your supervisors, you still need to recognize that because of their positions in the school setting they may at times direct your activities.

- **Identify who your immediate supervisor is for each of your assigned roles/responsibilities.**

With your primary supervisor, create a schedule of your various job responsibilities and make sure you are clear who your immediate supervisor is for each time period. Consider the following sample schedule of a paraeducator in an elementary school (see Figure 1.1).

Notice that this paraeducator has different

Figure 1.1

TIME	RESPONSIBILITY	IMMEDIATE SUPERVISOR
Before school	Supervise students eating breakfast in cafeteria.	Principal
8:45 to 10:00	Assist in 4th grade classrooms	Three 4th grade teachers
10:00 to 10:30	Supervise two recesses	Principal
11:00 to 11:30	Assist in office	Office Manager/Principal
11:30 to 12:30	Supervise in cafeteria	Principal
12:30 to 1:30	Assist in 5th grade classrooms	Three 5th grade teachers
1:30 to 2:30	Assist in 3rd grade classrooms	Two 3rd grade teachers
2:30 to 3:00	Assist in Math Lab	Math Lab teacher
3:00 to 3:30	Supervise bus loading	Principal

immediate supervisors throughout the day, depending on the time and the activity. When she is assigned to a particular classroom, it is the teacher in that classroom who is her immediate supervisor. For example, from 2:30-3:00, when the paraeducator assists in the Math Lab, the Math Lab teacher is her immediate supervisor.

The principal is her primary supervisor and the person she can go to for directions and/or questions regarding common area assignments (although he may or may not be physically present in those settings when she is supervising). As her primary supervisor, the principal is also the one she should go to should there be problems, for example, among the three 4th grade teachers when she is assigned to work with them.

NOTE: There may be additional complexity about who your supervisor is if you are assigned to work with an individual special education student all day. Even though you may go with this student to several different teachers' rooms, your primary supervisor—who is likely to be the student's "case manager" in this case—will ultimately be responsible for all that you do with the student.

• Interact appropriately with school staff.

When interacting with staff members who have more authority than you, you will need to find the appropriate levels of formality and familiarity. That is, while we recommend that you treat everyone in the school with dignity and respect (see Task 4), what constitutes respectful behavior with a friend or peer may not be appropriate when interacting with someone in a level of authority above you. Because the specifics will vary depending on each individual's particular situation, we simply recommend that you act a little more formal and take care not to act bossy, superior, or like a know-it-all with those who are higher in the hierarchy than you.

Whenever anyone higher in the school hierarchy makes a request of you or gives you a direction, you need to listen carefully and respond promptly and positively. This is especially true if the person is a supervisor. If you are asked to do something by a staff member who is not your supervisor and you aren't sure whether or not to comply or think that complying would mean

11

you couldn't carry out a previous instruction from your supervisor, explain that you need to check with your supervisor first. For example, if someone asks you to help with something at a time you are supposed to be somewhere else, respectfully say, "I would be glad to help with that, but I need to check with Mrs. Johnson, my immediate supervisor for that time, to make sure it is all right with her."

Hopefully this will never happen, but if someone asks you to do something that you think is a problem or wrong, be sure to check with your primary supervisor first. If your primary supervisor gives you permission, then you can go ahead. If you still think the action could be harmful to you or to a student, you can consider going to see the principal. You may also need to go to the principal if you have a problem with your primary supervisor and you have been unsuccessful in talking with him/her about it. Keep in mind that you only want to go to the principal if absolutely necessary and only for an extremely important problem.

(SPECIAL NOTE: If you ever need to see the principal, it's always a good idea to first ask the Office Manager or Secretary when it would be convenient for the principal to see you for a few minutes.)

- **Interact appropriately with those lower in the school hierarchy than you.**

Throughout this book, we will make specific suggestions on how you should interact with students. For now, just remember that the key to relating appropriately to those who have less authority than you is to not abuse the power you have.

PARA PROS WILL	WHEREAS PARA CONS TEND TO
• Listen carefully to directions.	• Only partially listen.
• Write down lengthy or complex directions.	• Do what they want regardless of directions.
• Ask questions to insure understanding.	• Argue about directions.
• Accept directions even if they do not think it is the best idea.	

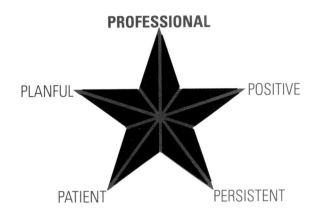

PROFESSIONAL

PLANFUL — POSITIVE

PATIENT — PERSISTENT

TASK 3:

Present yourself in a professional manner.

*A*lthough paraeducators are not generally considered part of a school's "professional" staff, it is important that you present yourself in a professional manner—that is, in a way that reflects positively on your school. This includes your appearance, your attitude, and your work habits.

Paraeducators sometimes report that students do not treat them with the same level of respect shown to teachers and administrators, which in turn can affect how effectively the paraeducators feel they are able to do their jobs. This may occur because those paraeducators look and act differently from the other adults on staff. We believe that when you dress and act in a professional manner, you will be more likely to get appropriate respect from the students.

In addition, the perceptions and attitudes of parents and other school visitors are influenced by the way all the members of a school's staff, including the paraeducators, look and act. When all staff members are neatly dressed and act in a knowledgeable, confident, and comfortable way, visitors will come away with a positive view of

the school. This holds true regardless of what the school building itself looks like.

HOW TO DO IT:

• Dress neatly and appropriately.

Whether or not you realize it (or like it), your appearance makes a statement about the respect you have for your job and affects the impression others—students, their families, fellow staff, and administrators—have of you. A paraeducator who is dressed in baggy sweat pants and a sweater with holes and coffee stains definitely gives the wrong impression. Therefore, one of the "basics" of being a successful paraeducator is to always come to school dressed neatly and cleanly. In addition, we suggest that you need to carefully consider the level of casualness/formality of your school attire. Overdressing can be as distracting and unprofessional as dressing sloppily.

Determining the appropriate degree of casualness/formality (e.g., Is a tie necessary? Are casual pants acceptable?) can only be done within the context of your particular school and community standards. In Kentucky, for example, one high

school principal told his staff, "If you don't change your clothes when you get home from work, then you weren't dressed for work." As a general rule, we recommend that you dress with a level of formality that is typical of most of the professional staff member(s) in your school. If you are unsure about what appropriate attire for your particular situation is, check with your primary supervisor.

• Act in a relaxed and confident way.

Notice that we did not say you need to be relaxed and confident, just that you should act relaxed and confident. In fact, there may be times when you are unsure of yourself or unsure

how to handle a situation. During such times, it is not necessary to give the impression that you know what to do when you don't. However, it is important to remind yourself that you provide a valuable service to your students and the community, and that you can solve any problem—eventually. Think about it like this: Would you rather go to a physician who bluffs and blusters when he is unsure about what to do or one who confidently says, "I am not sure about the best course of action, but I will find out."

In general, we suggest that you try to have your overall manner and actions reflect those of the majority of the people on your staff. That is, it's probably a good idea to avoid being the

PARA PROS WILL	WHEREAS PARA CONS TEND TO
• Act confidently, yet avoid coming off as either arrogant or shy. • Speak up, but avoid being the loudest person in any school setting.	• Convey over-confidence—maybe even creating the impression that they think they are better (smarter, younger, prettier) than other members of the staff. • Act loud and boisterous OR so timid and quiet that it appears she is trying to hide something.

loudest or the quietest staff member, the most or the least assertive staff member, the most or the least talkative staff member, the most or the least humorous staff member, and so on.

• Be a dependable and self-motivated employee.

The students and other staff members at your school count on you. It is important that you show up every day, arrive at work on time, fulfill your various duties without needing reminders, prepare in advance for instructional groups by looking over what you will be pre-senting, attend required meetings, stay on top of any paperwork or reports, and so on. With all of your assigned jobs, you need to do your very best. And, while we do not suggest doing jobs you have not been told to do, we do recommend making an effort to identify something that needs to be done if you find yourself with any "down" time. At that point, you should ask your immediate supervisor whether he or she would like you to do that task, or if there is something else that you should do.

REMEMBER, PARA PROS WILL:	WHEREAS, PARA CONS TEND TO:
• Come to work on time and as scheduled, unless they are truly sick.	• Stay home for the slightest reason.
• Be self-motivated and self-directed, and do their best at every task they are assigned.	• Require reminders and/or nagging to show up on time.
• Prepare in advance as much as is reasonably possible.	• Do only the bare minimum asked of them, and never try to prepare in advance.
• Avoid telling others how to do their jobs.	• Spend more time trying to boss others than doing their own work.

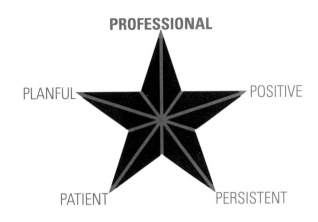

PROFESSIONAL

PLANFUL — POSITIVE

PATIENT — PERSISTENT

TASK 4:

Treat everyone in the school with dignity and respect.

B *eing respectful of the staff, students, and parents of students with whom you work is basic to being a successful paraeducator. Treating people with respect means demonstrating that you value them by, among other things, practicing simple politeness. It involves being a good listener, showing an active interest in them, and acknowledging their right to different opinions. Respect also includes recognizing that there are levels of authority in a school and accepting your own status within those levels. Treating the people in your school with respect is important simply because it is the right thing to do.*

There are also other reasons to make sure that respectful behavior is part of how you do your job. When you treat students with respect, you help them feel valued and you provide them with a model of how to treat others respectfully. When you treat parents and visitors with respect, you create a good impression of the school. Treating other paraeducators with respect is important for maintaining positive working relationships, and treating teachers and administrators with respect can be very important for your own job security. Last, but certainly not least, respectful behavior among a school's students, staff, and parents contributes significantly to ensuring a positive climate in that school.

The specific behaviors that will constitute respectful and disrespectful behavior in your school depend in part upon the standards of your community. For example, saying "Yes sir" and "Yes ma'am" is an important part of being respectful in some regions of the country (particularly when talking to someone in a higher level of authority), but is not considered necessary in other areas. Therefore, in the "How To Do It" section of this task, we offer some general guidelines regarding respectful behavior, as well as a series of considerations for you to think about and use to evaluate your own behavior. We strongly recommend that you make a point of taking time periodically throughout the school year to review these considerations.

HOW TO DO IT:

- **Demonstrate respectful behavior toward all people.**

Follow the Golden Rule: Do unto others as you would have them do unto you.

- **Demonstrate respectful behavior toward students.**

All your interactions with students should involve treating them with dignity and respect. That is, you want to do things like: speak to the student, not at the student; use the student's name frequently; give age appropriate praise; provide clear directions; correct errors (both academic and behavioral) with patience and persistence; use basic politeness (please, thank you, excuse me); smile and let your body language and tone of voice convey basic respect. You want to avoid letting frustration or anger with students spill over into disrespect, and you want to be careful about using teasing, humor (especially sarcasm), and nicknames. You are in a position of power with students—watch that you don't abuse that power.

Think honestly and objectively about how you treat students, particularly those students who misbehave and/or who struggle academically (i.e., make lots of mistakes). Ask yourself how you would feel if your supervisor did or said the same kinds of things to you, especially when the circumstances suggested that what you needed was more information about how to do your job appropriately. If you believe that having your boss treat you the way you treat students would make you feel valued and would help you learn what you needed to learn, then you probably are treating students respectfully. However, if you think you might be offended, hurt, or angry if your boss treated you that way, then you need to decide how you can be more respectful toward students and make a commitment to doing so.

- **Demonstrate respectful behavior toward teachers and administrators.**

When dealing with those in a higher position of authority in the school than you, you need to find the appropriate levels of familiar and friendly. As a general rule, we suggest that you use Dr., Mr., or Ms. and the person's last name, unless specifically told to use someone's first name. When you have a suggestion or an idea to share, be sure to present it in a way that does not sound too bossy or demanding.

Again, consider honestly and objectively how you act toward teachers, counselors, administrators, and others in your school who are in high-

er positions of authority than you. Now think about how you would feel if a student or a parent volunteer did or said the same kinds of things to you. If you would feel that the individual was being insulting, hostile, arrogant, overly familiar or friendly, or was in any other way failing to recognize the hierarchy of authority, you probably need to work on being more respectful toward those in positions of authority.

• Demonstrate respectful behavior toward fellow paraeducators.

When interacting with staff who are at or about your same authority level in the school, you need to find a balance. That is, you need to both avoid letting yourself be bullied or bossed around and refrain from trying to tell others how to do their jobs. Consciously value what paraeducators who have more experience, knowledge, or skills than you know; ask for ideas and suggestions. Make a point of developing collegial relationships with all your peers.

Now think honestly and objectively about how you act toward your peers. If you would be comfortable having them treat you in the same way, you are probably demonstrating appropriate respect. If, on the other hand, you would resent having a peer talk to or act toward you in a similar manner, then you need to think about modifying your actions. Remember, all the adults in the school need to work together if the school is going to accomplish its goals for students.

• Demonstrate respectful behavior toward parents and school visitors.

All parents and school visitors should feel welcome and important whenever they are on the school campus and/or interact with school staff. As you think honestly and objectively about your interactions with parents and visitors, ask yourself the following kinds of questions: Do you greet parents and visitors when you see them in the halls or when they come into an area where you are working? Do you let school visitors know that you are glad they are there and that you hope they have a pleasant visit? Are you careful not to project an air of superiority or self-importance around parents and visitors? If you cannot answer yes to these or similar questions, then you need to do a better job of treating parents and school visitors with respect.

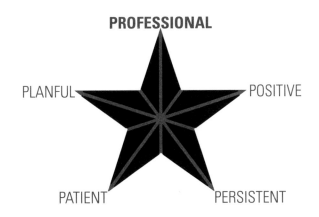

PROFESSIONAL

PLANFUL — POSITIVE

PATIENT — PERSISTENT

TASK 5:

Be aware of some basic school-based legal issues.

NOTE: The information in this task is a very simple introduction to some very complex and technical legal matters. It is not intended to constitute legal advice, but has been included to increase your awareness of some legal issues that affect students and staff in schools. You should plan on getting specific information on your school/district's legal policies and procedures from your primary supervisor or the building principal.

*A*s someone who works in a school, you need to be aware that legal issues may arise. Some basic knowledge and common sense can help you avoid situations in which you might get yourself or your school/district in trouble. First, know that activities that are illegal outside of school will be illegal in school as well. For example, if a school employee hits a child, that person can be accused of assault. Or, if a student accuses someone in a school of sexual impropriety, there will have to be an investigation. This may seem obvious, but you need to be very careful to never put yourself in a position where you could be accused of doing anything illegal.

Second, there are laws that are unique to school employees. For example, if you have any knowledge that a student is being abused or neglected and do not report it to your immediate supervisor or the building principal, you, your supervisors, and the school could face serious legal trouble. Also, as a paraeducator there is a high probability that at some time or another you will work with children identified as qualifying for special education services. An important federal law, called the Individuals with Disabilities Education Act (or IDEA, for short), dictates what schools must and cannot do in terms of these students.

The main purpose of IDEA is to ensure that schools provide all students who qualify for special education services with a "free appropriate public education" (or FAPE). It is important for you to be familiar with some of the essential aspects of IDEA—both to help you work more effectively with special education students and to help you avoid doing or saying anything that could result in the school district being out of compliance with the law. (That's a fancy way of saying that you have to be careful to avoid getting the district in legal hot water.)

NOTE: If you are ever unsure about any aspect of IDEA and how it affects you or your students, ask your primary supervisor or the special education teacher(s) in your school.

HOW TO DO IT:

- **Ask your primary supervisor OR building administrator for written copies of all district policies and procedures related to legal issues that you should know about.**

If there are no written guidelines, at least find out from your supervisor what you should do if you ever find yourself in any of the following situations:

—*You suspect that a child is being abused or seriously neglected.*

—*You suspect that a student is involved in illegal activity on school property (e.g., possession of a weapon or illegal drugs).*

—*You suspect that a student is involved in illegal activity off school property.*

- **If you are involved in or witness a situation that could potentially result in legal action, ask your building administrator if you should write notes about what occurred.**

If so, write the notes within a day or two of the incident (when the details are still fresh). Date and sign the notes, then give them to your administrator. For example, suppose you are supervising the playground when there is a fight and a student is injured. Ask the principal if she would like you to write a summary of the events. If this information is on file and the parents of the injured student file suit against the school, the principal will have a record that there were adults on duty and that the adults intervened at the ear-

liest possible time when the fight was observed. Once you have asked the principal whether to write notes, do not talk about the situation to anyone else. If someone such as a parent or an attorney contacts you, simply refer them to your primary supervisor or to the principal.

- **Be aware that IDEA (the federal law pertaining to students with disabilities) qualifies students in the following categories to receive special education services:**

Autism

Communication Disorder

Deaf/Blindness

Hearing Impairment

Mental Retardation

Orthopedic Impairment

Other Health Impairment

Serious Emotional Disturbance

Specific Learning Disability

Traumatic Brain Injury

Vision Impairment

NOTE: Your district/school may use slightly different terminology for their programs.

- **Be aware that IDEA (the federal law pertaining to students with disabilities) mandates that every student who receives special education and related services must have an Individualized Education Program (IEP).**

A student with severe emotional or behavioral problems may also have a Behavior Improvement Plan (BIP) as part of his/her IEP.

- **Be aware that IDEA (the federal law pertaining to students with disabilities) provides that school rules, policies, and procedures may have to be modified or adapted in order to meet the conditions of a student's IEP (Individualized Education Program).**

For example, a student on an IEP cannot be expelled from all school services for more than 10 days without reconvening the student's team to change his/her placement.

- **Be aware that under another federal law, §504, some students may be eligible for services whether or not they need special education.**

Ask your primary supervisor and administrator what information, if any, you need regarding §504.

- **Keep in mind that whenever you deal with a special education student, you need to defer to the special education teacher.**

This is the person who is responsible for ensuring that the student's IEP is appropriate and that it's implemented. If you have been assigned to help the special education teacher carry out the IEP for a student, do exactly what the teacher has specified—no more and no less. You can and should, however, provide any information you may have that might help the teacher make essential decisions. For example, if as you are working with the student you find that some aspect of the student's plan does not seem to be working in the student's best interest, discuss your concerns with the teacher. Do not make any modification in the plan without direction from the teacher.

- **Keep in mind that you should avoid sharing information about a student's progress with that student's parents, unless given specific directions by your supervisor to do so.**

You can facilitate communication between the parents and the school so each can get the information they want, but your involvement should always be guided by your supervisor.

- **Keep in mind that you should never give legal advice (or otherwise talk about the law) to students or parents.**

If a student or parent asks about some aspect of the law, refer them to the building principal or to the special education teacher.

- **Keep in mind that someone referred to as an "advocate" for a student may be helping the student's parent ensure that the student's legal rights are protected.**

If you are ever contacted by an "advocate," exercise caution. Do not talk with the individual, but refer him or her to the building principal or to your supervisor.

- **Remember that your primary supervisor and building administrator are your best sources of information regarding legal issues.**

RICO SEEMS TO BE MOVING AHEAD OF THE OTHER STUDENTS. DO YOU THINK IT MIGHT BE WORTH TRYING HIM IN THE GROUP WITH BETH AND RYAN?

NOTE: This task introduced a number of titles, acronyms, and definitions. The most important for you to remember is IEP (Individualized Education Program)—the plan that every student who qualifies for special education is required by law to have.

CHAPTER 1 | ACTIVITIES

THINK ABOUT IT

Use the following chart to evaluate your familiarity with the material presented in this chapter. When you have completed this activity, enter reminders about the tasks you wanted to reread or discuss into your planning calendar.

Figure 1.2 Reproducible Form

	The information was not applicable to my situation.	The information was familiar. I consistently implement the strategies presented.	The information was useful. I should reread this task at least once more this year.	Some of the information was new. I should reread this task within a month.	Much of the information was new. I should discuss it with my supervisor or with other paraeducators.
TASK 1: Remember the "bare essentials."	0	1	2	3	4
TASK 2: Understand the hierarchy of authority in your school	0	1	2	3	4
TASK 3: Present yourself in a professional manner	0	1	2	3	4
TASK 4: Treat everyone with dignity and respect	0	1	2	3	4
TASK 5: Be aware of some basic school-based legal issues	0	1	2	3	4

(NOTE: On pages 205-210, in the back of the book, you will find a complete chart of all the tasks in the book. You may wish to summarize the information from each individual chapter on this single chart.)

TAKE ACTION

For one full week, become an active seeker of useful information. Keep a notecard or blank piece of paper with you (in a pocket or on a clipboard). Whenever you hear a term or set of initials you are not familiar with, write it down. Note any school-related issue or question about the law and/or special education regulations about which you would like more information. Make a note if you find yourself unsure about the hierarchy of authority (e.g., you do not know who your immediate supervisor is in a particular situation). Remember, there are no "dumb" questions.

Arrange to meet with your primary supervisor at the end of the week. Ask your supervisor to answer the questions you have or help you find the information you need. Use the occasion to ask your supervisor for feedback about anything that you should be doing differently in order to be more effective in your job.

This process of identifying what you don't know and then seeking out the information demonstrates that you are trying to learn and grow in your role as paraeducator.

(NOTE: You may find this idea so useful that you will continue to keep a "Question" card handy even after this one-week activity.)

DISCUSS IT

Arrange with a group of colleagues to read Chapter 1 and do the Take Action activity for this chapter. Then schedule a meeting at which the group can discuss the following topics/questions.

1. Are there other "bare essentials" (in addition to those presented in Task 1) that should be shared with new paraeducators when they first start the job. (NOTE: You may wish to consider sharing these suggestions with your supervisor.)

2. Are the lines of authority in your school clear? If not, what might you do to help clarify this information?

3. Do students in your school treat the paraeducators with dignity and respect? If not, try to identify the reasons why. As a group, consider asking your primary supervisor or one or more of your immediate supervisors to discuss the problem with you and brainstorm possible remedies.

4. Discuss the information presented in Task 5: Be aware of some basic school-based legal issues. Pose questions to each other to see if you have the same understanding about the basics of the law and what it means in your job role. For example, someone might ask, "If a student tells me that he has not been fed dinner for the last two nights, do I report this to my supervisor as possible abuse?" If there are any issues or questions that the group cannot resolve/answer, arrange to ask your supervisor or the building principal for additional information.

5. Have each person share any useful ideas that were gained from working through the Take Action for this chapter.

CHAPTER 2

Being Part of the School Team

As a paraeducator, you are an important part of an organization (your school) with a huge responsibility—the education and well-being of hundreds of children. To successfully meet this responsibility, all of the adults in the school must work together as a team. Chapter 2 goes beyond the "basics" of being a paraeducator. The tasks in this chapter address attitudes and behaviors that will help you fit in, get along, and work more effectively with your fellow staff members as you all collaborate to educate the children you serve. That is, in this chapter you will learn how to be a positive member of the school team and how to contribute to a positive climate in your school.

As you review the tasks in this chapter, be sure to note which point(s) of the five-point star have been highlighted for each task.

Also, don't forget to check out the information presented by the Para-Pro and Para-Con characters!

27

The specific tasks in Chapter 2 are:

1. Demonstrate a positive attitude.

2. Use effective communication strategies.

3. Respect confidentiality.

4. Deal with disagreements productively.

5. Be responsible when it comes to meetings, workshops, and classes.

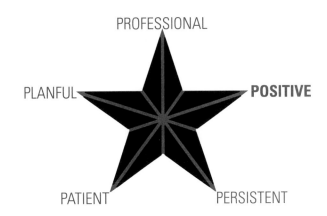

TASK 1:

Demonstrate a positive attitude.

Your attitude, positive or negative, has an impact on both how you act and how you feel. In fact, how you act affects how you feel, and how you feel affects how you act. When you act in a positive way (e.g., being friendly, greeting people, making positive comments, etc.), you are more likely to feel energetic, content, and upbeat—and when you feel energetic and upbeat, it is even easier to act in a positive way. Similarly, when you act in a negative way (e.g., being grumpy, scowling, making negative comments, etc.), you will tend to feel tired, frustrated, and unhappy. These negative feelings, in turn, will cause you to act even more negatively.

Demonstrating a positive attitude (and acting positively) is important for your own job satisfaction. Perhaps even more importantly, as a member of your school's "team" it is critical for you to have a positive attitude because your attitude and behavior affect the people around you. When you are positive, students and staff with whom you interact are more likely to be positive, and the opposite is true when you are negative. The fact is, your attitude has an impact on the climate of your school as a whole—contributing to the sense that the school is a place of happiness and joy rather than a place of apathy or drudgery.

HOW TO DO IT:

• Smile!

This may sound simplistic, but when you smile it actually makes you feel better. You don't have to be smiling every minute, but if you do not smile at least twice as much as you frown, you are probably making yourself (and the people around you) miserable. If you act like you are having a good time, you will start having a good time.

• Be polite, friendly, and helpful.

Try to make sure that each person with whom you interact (staff, student, parent, or visitor) feels as if he or she is very important to you.

— *Say "hello" to people.*

— *Ask how people are doing.*

— *Show an interest in people. "Gerilyn, How did that soccer game go?"*

— Use the word "please" when you make a request.

— Use the words "thank you" when a student does what you ask.

— Make a special effort to welcome parents and other visitors to the school.

— Convey an attitude of being willing to help out—to staff and students.

— Take the time to acknowledge staff for their help, suggestions, and guidance.

• **Look for and take advantage of opportunities to praise students.**

Observe students. When one or more students are doing what is expected of them, take the time to praise them for their independence and responsibility. Remember, praising students more than you correct them is one of the most important tools you have when dealing with student behavior.

(NOTE: We will provide more specific information on how to do this in the subsequent chapters.)

• **Keep a positive expectation for all the students with whom you work.**

You will undoubtedly deal with some students who have lots of problems and/or a long history of failure or misbehavior. However, you owe it to every student to communicate that you believe she or he can be successful. Make a point of looking for students' strengths rather than their weaknesses. Your positive expectations improve the likelihood that the students will actually meet those expectations.

• **Try to see the humor in different situations.**

Almost any situation has funny aspects to it. Look for opportunities to laugh. Laughter is like smiling. The physical act itself can have psychological effects. The key here is to have fun, but be respectful. That is, you want to avoid sarcasm, ridicule, or laughing at a student or group.

• **Leave your personal problems outside the school.**

This is not always the easiest thing to do, but if you are going through a tough time, try to mentally leave the problem behind when you

get to school. "My son and I had a big fight this morning and we will need to deal with it tonight. I will think about how I'm going to handle this when I drive home from work this afternoon. However, I am about to go in to work and I will not let my problem rub off on the kids or staff here at school." You are not only likely to have a better day at school, but you will quite possibly end up handling the problem better than if you had stewed on it all day.

- **When you are having a bad day and none of the suggestions above are working, do your best to get through the day, and tell yourself that tomorrow will be a better day.**

Remember to Smile

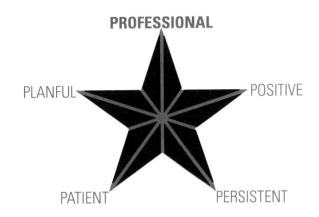

PROFESSIONAL

PLANFUL POSITIVE

PATIENT PERSISTENT

TASK 2:

Use effective communication strategies.

*I*n your work as a paraeducator, you will interact with students, staff, and perhaps parents. These interactions will inevitably involve communication. Communicating effectively means listening carefully (i.e., hearing and understanding) and speaking in clear, organized ways that make it easy for others to understand. Not all people are effective communicators. Some people may speak well, but even though they act like they are listening, what they hear is different from what the speaker is trying to convey. Other people may be good listeners, but they're not good communicators because they ramble or use jargon no one understands when they speak.

Effective communication is a critical, and complicated, skill. In fact, there are whole books (much longer and more technical than this one) that focus entirely on effective communication strategies. Because we feel that effective communication is so important for paraeducators, we have included it as a task in this chapter. Time and space constraints, however, allow us to focus on only two main aspects of effective com-

munication: a) active listening, in which you make a conscious effort to really hear what people are saying; and b) objective reporting, in which you talk or write about an individual or a situation by describing observable events and avoid jargon, labels, or conclusions.

Effective communication contributes to a school team's productivity and is respected and appreciated by school staff. Ineffective communication, on the other hand, can confuse and undermine the attempts of staff to fulfill the school's mission. When you make an effort to use effective communication strategies, you are demonstrating professionalism.

HOW TO DO IT:

- **Be an active listener when interacting with students as well as adults.**

Listening, like any other skill, is something that one can always improve. When you want to improve in a sport, you identify those aspects of the sport you do well and then you identify and work on (practice) those aspects that could use some fine tuning. Following are some keys to active listening. As you read through them, think about one or two areas that you could work on improving.

—Concentrate on the speaker and what is being said.

When you are talking with someone, keep your attention focused on what that person is saying. Don't let your mind wander to other things. Follow the ideas being presented. Some conversations may not require high levels of concentration. For example, if you and a couple of staff members are talking about your favorite football teams and the games you might watch over the weekend, it's probably not a problem if you have lapses in your concentration—as long as you're not rude. On the other hand, if your supervisor is telling you about techniques to use when working with a particular student, you need to be totally focused.

—Be alert for directions/instructions.

Listen for directions/instructions. Although some of your supervisors may be very clear about directions, others may tend to embed instructions in other things they are saying. If you are not careful, it can be easy to miss that you were told to do a particular task or handle a situation in a different way. As you listen to someone who tends to embed instructions, mentally highlight any sentences that include directions.

—Occasionally paraphrase what the speaker has said.

Paraphrasing is restating what was said, using different words. "So what you are saying is . . ." Paraphrasing demonstrates to the person speaking that you are really trying to understand what is being said, and it can help reduce misunderstandings. Don't just parrot back exactly what someone has said. If someone says she is angry, it doesn't help to say, "I hear you saying that you are angry." Paraphrasing should keep the conversation moving forward. When you paraphrase in a skillful way, the speaker will respond with something like, "Yes, that is exactly right, and what is also important is . . ." or "No, that's not it. What I meant was . . ."

Don't view the latter response as a failure or problem. Actually, it's a highly successful outcome because the paraphrasing prevented a misunderstanding.

—Ask questions when you do not understand something.

Remember, there's no such thing as a stupid question. When possible, ask a specific question. "So I should implement the time out procedure any time Thomas yells. What about if he uses a swear word?" When you don't have a specific question, but are somewhat confused, ask a general question such as, "Can you go over one more time how you want me to do that? I want to be sure I do it right."

—Notice the transitions between ideas.

Be aware of when the topic changes. That way, if you did not understand something from the previous idea, you can ask to go back to that topic. "Excuse me, Ruth, sorry for interrupting, but before we leave the topic of the new playground procedures, I want to be sure I understand something. Do we plan to . . ."

—Avoid rushing to judgment about what someone is saying.

It's not uncommon to start thinking you know exactly what someone is talking about before they have finished. Unfortunately, if you do this, you are likely to miss important information in the rest of what the person is saying. Using another sports example, this is like leaving a game at halftime because you think you know everything that's going to happen in the second half. However, this is rarely a safe assumption. As you listen to someone who is speaking, think of yourself as an information gatherer. Do not make judgments or draw conclusions until you have all the information.

—Maintain eye contact and use non-verbal cues to demonstrate that you are listening.

Part of active listening is making sure the person who is speaking knows you are listening. If you look bored or like your mind is elsewhere, the person speaking may assume you are uninterested—even if you really are concentrating. Don't use a robotic stare, but do look into the eyes of the speaker more frequently than you look elsewhere. In addition, occasionally nod your head to demonstrate agreement or understanding. If you are seated, you might want to lean forward slightly. (Leaning back can make you look so relaxed that you appear to be inattentive.)

- **Use objective reporting, especially when communicating about students or situations involving students.**

There are likely to be many occasions when your supervisor or building administrator will ask you to explain a situation or answer a question that involves a student. Following are examples of some of the kinds of things you might be asked to report on:

"Tell me about how Vernon is doing in his science class."

"How are things going at recess?"

"Is Maria improving her performance?"

"Tell me about the incident between Barry and Larry."

"What kind of week has Zach had?"

"How well is that small group behaving?"

In each of these cases, the individual making the request needs an objective, descriptive response if the information is going to be useful. Objective and descriptive responses describe events in concrete terms that explain what was seen or heard. This is in contrast to responses based on jargon, labels, and judgments—all of which are conclusions about, rather than observations of, events. Conclusions can be biased depending on whether you are having a good day, whether you like the student, or even whether you have some unconscious prejudices about a particular race, age level, or gender. Compare the responses shown in Figure 2.1 to the previous queries.

As you can see from the examples, while the non-objective responses may provide insight into what the person doing the reporting is thinking or feeling, they give very little information about what is actually going on with the students—and they could lead to confusion. On the other hand, the information provided in the objective descriptions is detailed and thorough enough to help a teacher or administrator get a more accurate picture of what has occurred.

Always try to be as specific and objective as possible in your verbal and written responses. Describe things that were actually seen and heard and avoid conclusions. As you read the following report, note how you can almost see and hear the scene unfold—and yet how it avoids drawing conclusions.

Kellen walked in the room, and as she walked by Justine's desk, she pushed the books off Justine's desk. Justine then said, "Kellen, get a life," and picked up her books. Kellen said, "You b——, I have a life." Justine said, "You may have a life, but I have Rob." Kellen then threw a book that hit Justine in the head. It all happened very

PARAPROS KNOW THAT THERE IS NO SUCH THING AS A STUPID QUESTION WHEN IT COMES TO MAKING SURE WE MEET THE NEEDS OF STUDENTS.

Figure 2.1

RESPONSES REFLECTING CONCLUSIONS	RESPONSES REFLECTING OBJECTIVE DESCRIPTIONS
"Vernon is really lazy."	"Vernon has completed one out of eight in-class assignments, and has turned in none of his homework."
"Recess is a zoo and the animals are out of control."	"This morning at recess I had to stop three fights. Many of the second grade students have begun doing some kind of chase game that is resulting in them running through games like four square and wall ball."
"Maria does not seem as learning disabled as she used to."	"Since we started the new procedures two weeks ago, Maria has gotten above 80% on seven out of seven of her assignments."
"Barry and Larry were angry and started fighting. I think it is a problem of racism."	"Barry and Larry were in a fight in which blows were exchanged and Larry was bitten on the arm. It took three adults to get them to stop. Larry made the following comments . . . ."
"Zach had a great week. He is such a wonderful kid."	"Zach completed all of his assignments and earned the full number of behavior points each day."
"The students in that small group are a bunch of spoiled brats."	"Four out of five students in the group are frequently off task. When given reminders, they pay attention for a few minutes, then they talk, look out the window, poke each other and so on."

quickly, before I had a chance to react. I told them both to stop, at which point I realized Justine was bleeding. I gave Justine a paper towel as a compress and told her to go with Beth to the health room. After giving Beth and Justine time to get out of the hall, I sent Kellen to the office with a referral marked "Physically Dangerous Behavior."

Objective reporting is easier if you use numbers whenever possible. Most of the objective responses in Figure 2.1 contained numbers. Following are some examples of ways to use numbers to describe students and their behaviors.

—*Use percentages when describing the quality of student work.*

"Her test scores on spelling tests have averaged about 60% to 65%, with the lowest test being 45% and the highest being 80%."

—*Count behaviors and use numbers to report the frequency with which a specific behavior occurred during a given time period.*

"During the reading period, she got out of her seat and had to be reminded to come back and sit down 4 times. Each time she was reminded, she did return to her seat."

—*Record and report the length of time a particular behavior occurs.*

(NOTE: A stopwatch is a very useful tool for reporting on behaviors that last a long time.)

"When given an instruction, the students take between 2 and 5 minutes before starting to carry out the instruction."

"The student was wandering around the room (when he was expected to be in his seat taking lecture notes) for 14 minutes."

NOTE: See Chapter 3, Task 6 for more details on collecting objective information.

PROFESSIONAL

PLANFUL · POSITIVE

PATIENT · PERSISTENT

TASK 3:

Respect confidentiality.

A school team can only truly function smoothly and effectively when there is a foundation of trust among its members. In addition to dependability (i.e., people doing what they say they will do), trust is built on individual members demonstrating respect for confidentiality. That is, the people you work with and for (i.e., staff, students, and students' families) need to know that you will not talk about them behind their backs and that you will not talk about sensitive school matters outside the school.

When someone fails to respect confidentiality, co-workers are likely to consider that person untrustworthy. In some cases, the co-workers may even try to avoid working with the person. Furthermore, the lack of confidentiality can lead to more than hurt feelings. In fact, failing to respect confidentiality can at times result in harm to an individual or even legal action against a school. Thus, those who engage in repeated and/or serious breaches of confidentiality risk losing their jobs.

As an employee with a commitment to professionalism and a member of your school's team, you need to be sure that you always respect the privacy and confidentiality of your co-workers, your students, and your students' families.

HOW TO DO IT:

• **Follow the Golden Rule.**

The most basic principle with regard to confidentiality is to not say anything to anybody about students or staff that you would not want someone saying about you or your family. A secondary principle is: If you are unsure about whether or not you should be talking about something, don't talk about it.

• **Never discuss students, staff members, or school problems with anyone outside the school.**

This may seem very blunt, but it is the standard. It is inappropriate for you to talk about people or problems related to your school outside the school setting. Not only might you be responsible for inadvertently passing along misinformation about an individual or a situation, but such a lack of respect for confidentiality almost always results in lowering the impression others have of the school. If someone persists in asking you about school related issues, politely inform the person that the building administrator might have more information. For example, you might say something like, "I really can't discuss that issue, Gracie. I can tell you that the staff members are great people who care about kids. If you think you need to know about this particular situation, you should call the principal and talk to her."

- **Never discuss students, staff members, or school problems with other school-based personnel if either you or they are not directly involved.**

Talking about school-related individuals or situations with other school personnel when one of you is not directly involved with the particular individual or situation is both unwise and unproductive. It's not likely that someone who is not directly involved in a situation can really contribute anything constructive to the matter and, unfortunately, in most work situations, there is the potential for rumors and gossip. It is important to avoid both of these. Thus, we recommend that you make it a practice to not discuss students, staff, or school problems with other staff members unless specifically asked to do so by your supervisor or building administrator.

- **Whenever it is necessary to discuss a school-related matter with other school personnel, keep your focus positive and productive, NOT negative.**

There certainly may be times when you will

be asked or need or want to talk about a student, a school problem, or possibly even a staff member, with another member of the school staff. The critical issue in these instances is to be positive and constructive (i.e., focus on productive action) rather than negative (i.e., focus on unproductive complaining). For example, if you need to talk to your supervisor about a problem with a student, you should say something like, "Mr. Alexander, I am having trouble with Marco. He seems really angry all the time and I am wondering if you can give me some ideas on how to help him" rather than, "Marco is driving me crazy. He is so annoying!"

If you are having difficulty with a particular staff member, the most appropriate response is to discuss your concern directly with that individual—NOT to talk about that person to someone else. In Task 4 of this chapter, you will find more information on dealing with disagreements productively.

Finally, if you find yourself uncomfortable about a particular situation, first ask yourself whether it negatively impacts students. If it does, then go to the person involved or to an appropriate authority—generally your primary supervisor or your building administrator. Remember to present your concerns thoughtfully and respectfully. If the situation does not affect students or is a minor annoyance or is something you know you cannot change, the best policy is to keep your opinion to yourself and accept the situation without complaining.

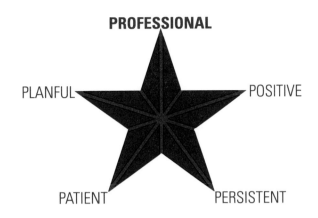

PROFESSIONAL

PLANFUL

POSITIVE

PATIENT

PERSISTENT

TASK 4:

Deal with disagreements productively.

In any organization where people work together, disagreements are going to happen. A disagreement does not have to be a problem. In fact, disagreements can actually be healthy because they provide an opportunity for people to work together to find the best solution to an issue or problem.

In your work as a paraeducator, there will undoubtedly be times when you will disagree with someone. In some of these instances you will be in the "right" and in some (this may be hard to imagine) you will be in the "wrong." What is important is not to try to avoid all disagreements, but to handle any disagreements that may occur, professionally.

HOW TO DO IT:

- **Keep your focus on what is best for students.**

When a disagreement occurs, consider the needs of the students. If you keep your focus on what is best for students, you will not fall into the trap of engaging in disagreements just to be disagreeable, or to "get under the skin" of some-

one you don't like, or to show off, or to exert power. In general, we suggest that if a disagreement does not directly affect students one way or another, you are better off not getting too involved.

- **Be positive, calm, and respectful during any disagreement.**

It may not always be easy, but it is possible (and preferable) to be pleasant and to maintain positive relations when disagreeing with someone. It is even more critical to treat someone with whom you are disagreeing, respectfully. Again, this may be difficult, but you want to try to avoid feeling so convinced you are right that you fail to really listen to what the other person has to say. Recognize that he or she may be right or that, even if wrong, the person is probably doing the very best he or she can at that moment. Never engage in name calling, shouting, or in making accusations such as, "Well if you really cared about our students you would . . . ." Make an effort to use "I messages" to communicate your position (e.g., statements beginning with phrases such as "I think . . . ." or "What I have noticed is . . . ."). Monitor your body language. Strive to find the balance between assertively communicating your position and avoiding being either overly aggressive or completely passive. Whenever you interact with someone remember to use language that consists of objective descriptions rather than labels, judgments, or jargon and to engage in active listening. Finally, remember not to discuss a disagreement you have with one staff member with others who are not involved.

• Proceed cautiously when disagreeing with someone in a higher position of authority.

Disagreeing with someone in a position of authority over you can be somewhat tricky. The first thing to consider is whether you are directly or indirectly responsible to that individual. In general, when you disagree with someone in a position of direct authority over you (e.g., your primary supervisor), carefully consider all the consequences before taking any action.

Remember that it is the responsibility of the teachers and administrators at your school to make decisions and your responsibility to do what you are asked to do. If you are troubled by a particular decision, one way to communicate your concern is to frame your opinion in the form of a question. For example, you might ask something like, "Do you think it might be all right if I did _____ instead?" Once a decision has been made, however, you need to carry it out—no disagreements, no questions. Again, one of the "basics" of being a successful paraeducator is to follow instructions.

If you feel *strongly* that students are being hurt (physically, emotionally, or educationally) by a particular policy or procedure and you have tried unsuccessfully to communicate your concerns to your immediate and/or primary supervisor, you will have to decide whether or not to talk to the school principal about the

matter. Before you take that step, ask yourself whether you can show how students are being harmed. If not, don't do it. If you can, be sure to present your position in a constructive rather than critical manner.

There also may be times when you disagree with an individual who has more authority than you in general (e.g., a teacher or a counselor), but who is not your supervisor. For example, you may be asked by a teacher other than your supervisor to do a task that you think is not part of your job responsibilities. As a basic rule, we recommend: If you have the time, do whatever someone with more authority asks you to do. This is part of being a member of the school team. However, if you are asked to do something that will interfere with your assigned responsibilities, politely inform the person making the request that you will be glad to help, but that you must first carry out the expectations of your supervisor. Consider the following examples.

1) You are assigned to work with a third grade teacher from 9:00 to 10:00 and a fifth grade teacher from 10:00 to 10:30. At 9:50, the third grade teacher asks you to escort her class down to the cafeteria for a schoolwide assembly scheduled from 9:55 to 10:15. She further instructs you to stay with the students and bring them back to the classroom when the assembly is over. An appropriate response would be to politely say, "I would be happy to do that, but from 10:00 to 10:30 Mrs. Reston is my supervisor. Would you please check with her? If she tells me to stay with your class, I'd certainly be willing to do so."

2) You are copying papers for your supervisor, the special education teacher. He needs these papers for an important meeting that will be taking place soon. Another teacher comes by, sets a bunch of papers down, and tells you to copy them immediately. You realize that if you copy the papers for her, you may not be able to get the papers to your supervisor on time. An appropriate response in this

situation would be to respectfully say, "Mr. Younce has asked me to get these papers ready for a meeting at 3:00. If I copy the papers for you, I'm not sure I will be able to complete the task Mr. Younce has assigned to me." If the other teacher persists in demanding you copy her papers, politely ask her to talk to Mr. Younce about what you should do.

Note that in both examples, we do not suggest that you refuse to carry out the task of the individual who is not your supervisor. As a paraeducator, you should always be prepared to respect the fact that in the school setting, teachers direct your activities. However, you also can and should be clear that the expectations of your supervisor take precedence. Please notice as well, that we recommend you avoid putting yourself in the position of having to ask your supervisor which task you should perform. That is, whenever possible, ask the person making the second request to speak directly to your supervisor. This reduces the possibility of your being caught in the middle between two members of the professional staff.

- **Proceed thoughtfully when disagreeing with someone at the same or a lower level of authority.**

If you disagree with another paraeducator who is on the same level of authority as you about something, the best approach is to try to resolve the situation by talking it out and exploring different options with that person. If the two of you cannot agree, you then need to decide whether you believe the issue is one that absolutely needs to be resolved. (Remember, there are some situations in which the parties can agree to disagree.) If you determine that the issue must be resolved, ask your co-worker if he or she would be willing to discuss the situation with your supervisor and let the supervisor decide. If the other person refuses, you may need to present the situation to the supervisor yourself and ask his/her advice. For example, consider two paraeducators who are assigned to supervise the cafeteria and who disagree about how they are to excuse students. If they are unable to resolve the issue by talking it through themselves, they should make an appointment with the primary supervisor for cafeteria duty to present their respective positions. Keep in mind that once you choose to involve a supervisor, you must be prepared to follow through, with grace and dignity, on any decision that supervisor makes. That is, do not gloat or brag if the decision goes "your way," nor whine or pout if it does not.

If your disagreement involves someone who is under your authority (e.g., because you have more experience and seniority or because you have been assigned to train the person), be careful not to abuse the power you have been given. If the individual has failed to do something that you have asked him/her to do, start by restating your expectation and the reason for the expectation. If the person still fails to comply, consult with your primary supervisor or building principal about how to proceed. Do not argue with or try to bully the person.

• Follow through on any decisions made.

Once a decision has been made, you must follow through on the provisions of that decision whether or not you agree with it. Be very careful to never do anything that might sabotage a decided-upon policy or procedure. For example, if you are assigned to supervise the cafeteria during lunch and school staff decides to change the procedure for dismissing students from the cafeteria, you must do everything possible to make that new procedure work for students—even if you do not think the change is a good one.

- **Proceed effectively when disagreeing with a student.**

The most common kind of disagreement you are likely to encounter is one involving a student. That is, you may frequently be in the position of asking students to do things they do not particularly want to do (e.g., "Get back to work" or "Walk, do not run, in the hall"). Handling student "disagreements" of this kind will be discussed specifically in the next chapter. For now, the following suggestions may help you avoid disagreements with students:

—*Give clear directions (that tell students what to do rather than what not to do).*

—*Give only one direction at a time.*

—*Use the student's name when giving a direction.*

—*Use a clear, calm voice when giving a direction.*

—*If the student fails to comply, tell the student that he or she is not following directions and repeat the direction.*

—*Do not argue with the student.*

—*If the student continues not to comply, get the student's name (or somehow be able to identify the student).*

—*Bring any concerns about insubordination to the attention of your supervisor.*

- **Remember, whatever the nature of a disagreement, once it has been resolved, LET IT GO!**

Para-Cons may act like they agree with a decision, and then do exactly what they want to do regardless of policy or directions. They may even try to sabotage decisions/policies they do not like.

PROFESSIONAL

PLANFUL • **POSITIVE**

PATIENT • **PERSISTENT**

TASK 5:

Be responsible when it comes to meetings, workshops, and classes.

*A*s a paraeducator, you may at times be asked/required to attend meetings, workshops, and/or classes. Being part of the school team means that you need to exhibit the same kind of responsible and appropriate behavior toward these important activities as you do toward your everyday job tasks.

The purpose of most school-related meetings is to allow staff members (as well as parents and/or others) to share information and ideas, discuss issues, and possibly make group decisions. When you are asked to attend a meeting, it is probably because your building principal or primary supervisor feels you would benefit from learning more about the meeting's topic(s). It is also very likely that he or she wants you there because you can contribute a unique perspective on the matter.

Workshops and classes, on the other hand, are usually designed to increase the knowledge or skills of the attendees. If you are asked or required by your school or district to attend a workshop or class, there is probably an expectation that you will use the information or skills

taught in the session. In other words, workshops and classes represent opportunities for professional development.

Your attitude toward and behavior during a meeting, workshop, or class will have a direct impact on how much you personally will get out of the session—which, in turn, will affect the overall climate and success of the meeting, workshop, or class.

HOW TO DO IT:

- **Approach meetings, workshops, and classes with a positive attitude.**

It is critical to go into any meeting, workshop, or class with the idea that the content to be covered will be worthwhile and useful. If you start with the assumption that a session will be a waste of time, you are likely to miss out on information or strategies that could help you do your job more easily or effectively.

- **Arrive at meetings, workshops, and classes on time and with all necessary materials.**

Failing to arrive at a session on time reflects both a lack of professionalism and a lack of respect. Showing up without some means of taking notes gives the impression that you assume nothing worth reviewing later will occur during the session. At the very least, come to meetings, workshops, and classes with a pen or pencil and some paper (preferably a notepad). If the session is a continuation of a class or previous meeting, bring your notes from any earlier session(s) and/or any completed assignment(s) that may be due. If the workshop or class uses a textbook or other material, bring that with you as well.

- **Be courteous and participate actively during meetings, workshops, and classes.**

Courteous behavior during meetings, workshops, and classes is very simple. It means giving anyone who is speaking to the group your full attention, not talking while someone else is talking, coming back from breaks on or before the designated time, and not leaving until the meeting is over or you have been dismissed. Courteous behavior also involves carefully considering whether it is necessary and appropriate to publicly disagree with what is being presented. If you feel that it is important to correct some misinformation or voice your opinion, do so respectfully. Raise your hand, wait to be called upon, and then state what you have to say without insulting or attacking the person with whom you disagree. DO NOT express your disagreement by rolling your eyes, passing notes, sighing, or looking disgusted.

Active participation involves looking at the individual who is speaking, occasionally nodding your head to let the speaker know you are paying attention, keeping your attention focused when assigned a task (e.g., you are asked to discuss something in small groups), and writing down any information that you will want/need to review later. (Hint: Figure out a way to flag any part of your notes that discusses direct action required by you. For example, you might put an * in the margin next to any note that should be put on your list of things to do or in your planning calendar.)

Active participation means asking questions

PARA-PROS WILL:	WHEREAS, PARA-CONS TEND TO:
• Participate actively, but not attempt to be the "star" of the show. • Ask appropriate questions for clarification or more information.	• Share too many personal stories. • Go on and on and on and on and on . . . . • Ask too many questions. • Never ask a question, even when they are confused about something or need more information.

when you need clarification or do not understand something. If you do need to ask a question, make sure it is designed to help clarify an area of misunderstanding and/or to seek additional information. Some people ask questions to try to put the speaker on the defensive. Some people ask questions to hear the sound of their own voice. Some people ask questions, but are really trying to get their own opinion across. None of those represents appropriate participation.

Finally, active participation includes providing honest and helpful feedback on evaluation forms at the conclusion of a class or workshop. If you have concerns or criticisms, present them constructively. And don't forget to note the positives. Taking the time to identify what specifically about a class you found useful (and why) is not only beneficial to the presenter/sponsor of the workshop, but also increases the probability that you will incorporate the new information/strategies into your daily actions.

• **Follow through on meetings, workshops, and classes by implementing decisions made and/or new skills learned.**

If you attend a staff meeting where a decision is made regarding a change in policy or procedure, be prepared to apply that decision without reminders or nagging. For example, if staff decide on a new procedure for dismissing students from the cafeteria, you should begin using the new procedure on the identified start date.

When you attend a class at which a new procedure is presented, think about how you could implement the procedure, but talk to your supervisor before you actually do so. That is, the decision of whether and when to implement any new procedure or technique needs to be made by someone in a position of authority. This is especially important if the situation involves students who qualify for special education services.

CHAPTER 2 ★ ACTIVITIES

THINK ABOUT IT

Use the following chart to evaluate your familiarity with the material presented in this chapter. When you have completed this activity, enter reminders about the tasks you wanted to reread or discuss into your planning calendar.

Figure 2.2 Reproducible Form

	The information was not applicable to my situation.	The information was familiar. I consistently implement the strategies presented.	The information was useful. I should reread this task at least once more this year.	Some of the information was new. I should reread this task within a month.	Much of the information was new. I should discuss it with my supervisor or with other paraeducators.
TASK 1: Demonstrate a positive attitude.	0	1	2	3	4
TASK 2: Use effective communication strategies.	0	1	2	3	4
TASK 3: Respect confidentiality.	0	1	2	3	4
TASK 4: Deal with disagreements productively.	0	1	2	3	4
TASK 5: Be responsible when it comes to meetings, workshops, and classes.	0	1	2	3	4

(NOTE: On pages 205-210, in the back of the book, you will find a complete chart of all the tasks in the book. You may wish to summarize the information from each individual chapter on this single chart.)

TAKE ACTION

For one full day, monitor the degree to which you respect confidentiality. That is, as you go about your duties, identify any occasion when you talk about students, families, or other staff with someone who has no professional need for the information. At the end of the day, if you have had no lapses in confidentiality, congratulate yourself on your professionalism. If there was a lapse or two, make a commitment to change your behavior and mentally rehearse how you can avoid such a problem in the future. Set a date to do this activity again in a couple of weeks. If you found there was a particular situation about which you had a question (e.g., Is this situation something I could share with my husband?), discuss it with your supervisor.

(NOTE: You may have a tendency to shrug off this suggestion, believing that you always respect confidentiality. However, we strongly encourage you to spend one day "looking over your own shoulder" to ensure that you are as respectful of confidentiality as you think you are.)

On another day, monitor your attitude—to determine whether it is generally positive or negative. Observe, and perhaps even make notes about, how much of the time during the day you present an optimistic and upbeat demeanor. If it is less that 75% of the day, plan to spend a week working on implementing the suggestions from Task 1: **Demonstrate a positive attitude.**

DISCUSS IT

Arrange with a group of colleagues to read Chapter 2 and do the **Take Action** activity for this chapter. Then schedule a meeting at which the group can discuss the following topics/questions.

1. Identify some major factors about being a paraeducator that make it difficult to have a positive attitude. Discuss how you might maintain a positive attitude while dealing with these factors. NOTE: *Do not* let this turn into a gripe session and do not violate confidentiality by referring to any students, families, or staff members by name. Keep the focus on how you, as paraeducators, can keep positive. Remember that the only thing you have full control over is yourself—that is, you *can* manage your own attitude.

2. Have each person take a turn describing a student's behavior. The other members of the group should give feedback if the description veers into jargon, labels, or conclusions, and help the person restate that portion of the description in objective terms.

3. Discuss the issue of confidentiality. For example, you might consider questions such as:

   —*What can you share with your own family about how your day went without violating confidentiality?*

   —*What can you share with an acquaintance who asks, "What is involved in being a paraeducator and do you like your job?"*

4. Review the suggestions in Task 4 regarding how to deal with disagreements productively. Have each person identify one way in which he or she currently deals with disagreements well and one way in which he or she needs to improve. Note that each person should identify only his or her *own* strengths and weaknesses—not someone else's. If an individual chooses, he or she might ask the group to help brainstorm ideas and suggestions for how to go about improving in a specific area. This could include role playing a situation to demonstrate or practice the ideas/suggestions.

5. Have each person share any useful ideas that were gained from working through the **Take Action** activity for this chapter.

CHAPTER 3

Managing Student Behavior

As a paraeducator, it is highly likely that you will work directly with students. And, as anyone who deals with children will tell you, behavior and discipline can sometimes be a challenge. There are likely to be times when a student or a group of students will test limits, act silly, or even display overt disrespect or defiance. The six tasks in this chapter present information designed to help you deal more effectively with student behavior.

SPECIAL NOTE: This chapter includes basic concepts and general guidelines for managing student behavior. Chapters 4, 5, 6, and 7 provide information and strategies for applying these concepts and guidelines in the following specific situations:

- *Supervising common areas (e.g., playground, cafeteria)*

- *Working with small groups*

- *Supervising independent work periods*

- *Working with an individual student*

The specific tasks in Chapter 3 are:

1. Become familiar with some basic concepts related to behavior.

2. Be clear about what is expected of the students and what is expected of you.

3. Actively monitor student behavior.

4. Reinforce responsible student behavior.

5. Respond to (correct) irresponsible student behavior in ways that will help students learn to behave more responsibly.

6. Understand some basic concepts related to information-based decision making.

7. Prevent (and/or deal effectively with) student non-compliance.

Don't forget—as you read Chapter 3, keep an eye out for the five-point stars and the information presented by the Para-Pros and Para-Cons.

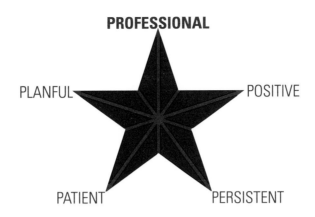

PROFESSIONAL

PLANFUL — POSITIVE

PATIENT — PERSISTENT

TASK 1:

Become familiar with some basic concepts related to behavior.

$\mathcal{Y}$*ou will be able to manage student behavior more effectively if you have a basic understanding of behavior and how it can be modified. In this task, we present some "big picture" concepts related to that topic. We have highlighted the "Professional" point on the five-point star because it is up to you to make sure that you understand and actually use this information as you work with students to help them behave more responsibly. (NOTE: Since the task itself is to learn the information, there is no "How To Do It" section.)*

• First Important Concept: Behavior is learned.

People are constantly engaged in learning. For example, if you purchase a car and you like the way it drives, find it never needs repairs, and believe you got a good value for what you paid, then you are more likely to buy that make of car in the future. On the other hand, if you discover that the car handles poorly, needs constant repairs, and was overpriced, you are not likely to buy that make of car again. Or, if you go to a movie based on a friend's recommendation, but find it to be a poor movie and a waste of your money, you are less likely to ask for that friend's movie recommendations in the future.

Scenarios such as those are repeated in each person's life many times a day—in uncountable, interwoven combinations—to create a rich fabric of experiences and learning. Simply put, a person's behavior is influenced by the conditions and events that he or she experiences. Some of these events and conditions serve to encourage the person to engage in certain behaviors, while others discourage the person from engaging in certain behaviors. The following model (Figure 3.1) shows the relationship among the three main variables that affect behavior.

Those with behavioral training will recognize this model as an illustration of behavioral theory—expressed in common sense and practical terms. Basically, the model suggests that when your goal is to eliminate undesirable behavior and/or foster desirable behavior, you need to

VARIABLES THAT AFFECT BEHAVIOR

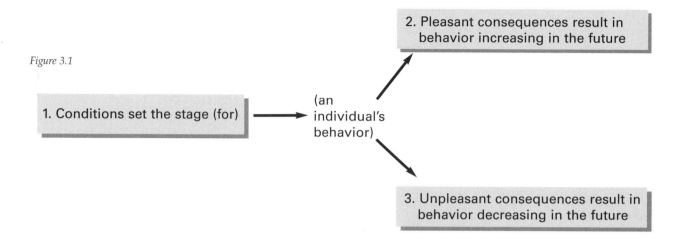

Figure 3.1

consider and address: a) conditions that prompt the behavior to occur; b) events following the behavior that make it more likely the behavior will occur again (pleasant consequences); and c) events following the behavior that make it less likely the behavior will occur again (unpleasant consequences).

The other important idea to keep in mind as you consider this model is that what may be "pleasant consequences" for one person could be "unpleasant consequences" for another. For example, getting a smiley-face sticker for having done good work is likely to be a pleasant consequence for a first grader—something that will encourage (or reinforce) him or her to work hard in the future. However, the same thing may very well have an opposite effect on a tenth grader. That is, getting a sticker for having done good work may be so embarrassing to a tenth grader that he or she will be less likely to work hard in the future.

- **Second Important Concept: Any behavior that occurs repeatedly is serving some function for the individual exhibiting the behavior.**

The idea that any chronic behavior serves a function is essential to keep in mind as you strive to help students behave responsibly. Students who consistently behave responsibly have learned that responsible behavior leads to

things they value, such as parental approval, good grades, teacher attention, a sense of pride and accomplishment, and so on. Their responsible behavior serves a function.

However, this concept applies as much to behaviors that are negative or destructive as it does to behaviors that are positive and productive—which helps explain an individual student's behavior when the consequences of that behavior seem so unpleasant. For example, consider Rex, a seventh grade student who chronically argues with staff (and has since he entered middle school). Rex is frequently sent out of class and assigned detention, his parents are called regularly, and school staff are continually angry and frustrated with him. Yet, as unpleasant as these consequences appear to be, Rex is getting some benefit from his irresponsible behavior or he would change it.

In Rex's case, his misbehavior results in consequences that are pleasant (or positive) for him. That is, when he argues, he gets lots of attention (direct and angry engagement) from adults—which gives him a sense of power. In addition, he gets lots of attention from peers for appearing strong and powerful enough to "fight" with teachers. Rex's irresponsible behavior also allows him to avoid some unpleasant (or negative) consequences that result when he exhibits responsible behavior. That's because Rex has academic problems. When he tries to be compliant and do his work, he usually finds that he can't do it, which frustrates and discourages him. Rex has discovered that if, instead of doing his work, he argues and gets thrown out of class, he not only gets adult and peer attention, but he also avoids having to publicly demonstrate his lack of academic ability.

When a student frequently behaves irresponsibly, it's likely the student hasn't experienced the benefits (i.e., pleasant/positive consequences) of responsible behavior frequently or powerfully enough. It's also likely that student has learned that irresponsible behavior is a more effective and/or efficient way of getting his/her needs met (e.g., the student gets power, control, and perhaps even admiration from peers)—that is, the irresponsible behavior serves a function.

- **Third Important Concept: Behavior can be changed.**

Although it is true there are some tendencies or personality traits that seem to be present from birth, it is very important to understand that most behavior is learned—which means it can be unlearned. Consider the following rather exaggerated example.

Picture Cindy—a very responsible, successful, and kind sixth or seventh grade student. Imagine that, as of today, Cindy stops getting any positive benefits for behaving responsibly. She does her best work, but only gets failing grades and critical comments. The other students laugh at her work and class participation, and even ridicule her as stupid. Her parents show no interest in the fact that she is failing. Although she tries to be nice to adults and other students, they are no longer nice in return. She stays on task, but no one ever notices. Neither the adults at school or at home comment on her effort, her independence, her cooperation, or her kindness. Instead, they constantly demand more and more and appear to look for every opportunity to scold and criticize (think of Cinderella's treatment by her stepfamily). If this were to continue day after day, at home and at school, there is an excellent chance that eventually Cindy would stop trying to be kind and responsible.

It's possible she would begin to respond with anger and hostility. Should Cindy find that acting in an antagonistic and aggressive manner was a way to get people to notice her and "get people off her back," she might even develop a sense of satisfaction or self-preservation in behaving that way. If the situation were to continue for months or years, you would likely have a very different young woman from the one first described. Fortunately, this scenario is very unlikely.

Now, think back to Rex, the student who is always argumentative, angry, and getting thrown out of class. Imagine what would happen if school personnel created a situation in which he started experiencing academic and behavioral success (e.g., getting good grades, receiving peer recognition for his appropriate behavior) and he no longer received a lot of attention or status for his anger and hostility. If done well (i.e., consistently and for a sustained length of time), the school could create a powerful positive change in Rex's behavior (in the exact opposite direction of Cindy's).

The point is: Behavior can be taught and changed!

- **Fourth Important Concept: When working to change behavior, focus more energy on encouraging responsible (desired) behavior than on trying to reduce inappropriate behavior.**

As noted in the Introduction to this chapter, in your work as a paraeducator, you are likely to encounter student misbehavior. When an individual student regularly has behavior problems, school staff may work together to create an intervention or Behavior Improvement Plan (BIP) for that student. Although you are not likely to be asked to design a BIP, you may be asked to help implement one. Following is a sample Behavior Improvement Plan that might have been designed for Rex, our hypothetical student who has a problem with arguing (Figure 3.2). We have included this sample plan to help you better understand why you may be asked to do certain things when working with a student who has behavioral problems.

You will note that the five categories in the plan address the three main variables represented in the behavioral model shown in Figure 3.1 (page 58). Notice, also, that the specific procedures included in each category focus more on encouraging responsible behavior than on punishing misbehavior. That is because emphasizing positive rather than punitive procedures is more effective.

Implementing an intervention plan that addresses all five categories and focuses more on encouraging responsible behavior than on pun-ishing irresponsible behavior increases the probability that efforts to help the student learn to behave more responsibly will be successful. The sample plan for Rex, for example, would be far less effective if staff did not pay attention to eliminating the positive aspects of exhibiting the irresponsible behavior-getting adult attention and getting attention from peers. In fact, Rex's behavior would not be likely to improve if he could still get lots of peer and adult attention through arguing, because for him the benefit of getting peer and teacher attention may outweigh any benefits from the other positive procedures that have been included.

Figure 3.2

SAMPLE BEHAVIOR IMPROVEMENT PLAN
FOR REX BRADY

1. Modify conditions (e.g., schedule, physical structure, organization, and so on) to prompt more responsible behavior from the student.

   • Give Rex a high status job (to be performed daily) that will increase his sense of power and purpose in the school.

   • Give Rex lessons on respect; specifically, teach him how to disagree, make requests, state a position, and so on without arguing.

   • Arrange for Rex to receive private tutorial assistance in his most difficult academic subjects.

   • Prompt staff to always give Rex very clear directions.

   • Remind staff to avoid power struggles with Rex.

   • Ask all staff to give Rex frequent non-contingent attention (e.g., say "hello" to him; smile at him, etc.).

2. Implement effective "reinforcement" procedures that are likely to encourage the student to exhibit more responsible behavior in the future.

   • Remind staff to praise Rex privately when he follows directions without arguing.

3. Eliminate unpleasant/negative consequences that may discourage the student from exhibiting responsible behavior in the future.

   • Have teachers modify Rex's assignments to decrease the possibility that Rex will get frustrated and discouraged when doing academic work.

   • Have teachers preteach Rex particularly difficult assignments to decrease the possibility that he will get frustrated and discouraged when doing academic work.

   • Prearrange times during the day when Rex can privately ask teachers questions and/or get assistance to decrease the possibility that he will feel embarrassed in front of peers.

   • Remind staff to avoid publicly praising Rex for following directions to decrease the possibility that Rex will feel embarrassed in front of peers.

Figure 3.2 (Continued)

SAMPLE PLAN (CONTINUED)

4. Eliminate any pleasant/positive consequences that may encourage the student to exhibit irresponsible behavior in the future.

  • Train staff to NOT engage in arguing with Rex, so he does not get undue adult attention for misbehavior.

  • Train staff to maintain instructional momentum, so Rex will not get undue attention from peers when he attempts to argue.

5. Implement effective "correction" procedures that are likely to discourage the student from exhibiting irresponsible behavior in the future.

  • Inform all staff to consistently respond to Rex's misbehavior in the following way:

    a. Give a warning—that is, label the behavior (e.g., "That is arguing.")—when Rex starts to argue.

    b. Calmly implement a corrective consequence (e.g., assign time-owed) if Rex continues to argue after the warning.

    c. Ignore any further attempts by Rex to engage in arguing.

PROFESSIONAL

PLANFUL · POSITIVE

PATIENT · PERSISTENT

TASK 2:

Be clear about what is expected of the students and what is expected of you.

The more planful you can be about the situations in which you will be working, the more successful you will be at managing student behavior (and doing your job generally). One of the most important planning methods you have is to ask your immediate supervisor(s) for each particular assignment exactly what is expected of the students and what is expected of you in that situation.

The information about the expectations for students is important so that you will know what student behaviors to watch for, which behaviors are to be reinforced or encouraged, and which behaviors are to be corrected. For example, you need to know whether it is acceptable behavior for a student to leave her seat during independent seatwork to sharpen her pencil. If it is acceptable, and the student behaves responsibly and gets back on-task immediately, that behavior should be encouraged with a smile or even verbal praise. On the other hand, if students are expected to get permission before getting out of their seats, this student's actions

would be a minor misbehavior that should be corrected.

The information about what is expected of you is important so that you will know, among other things, how your supervisor wants you to monitor student behavior, reinforce or encourage responsible student behavior, and respond to or correct irresponsible student behavior. Other important information you will need in order to do your job well includes what your responsibility is for communicating the behavioral expectations to students, how you should deal with emergencies, and what, if any, additional responsibilities you may have in each situation.

The expectations for students and for you are likely to vary from setting to setting, from activity to activity, and from supervisor to supervisor. For example, say you work in a particular teacher's classroom for an hour each day. During the first 30 minutes of the hour, you provide extra reading practice to a small group of students. During the second half-hour, you supervise students who are doing independent seatwork, while the teacher works with a small group of students. What is expected of the students and what is expected of you will likely be different during the small group reading practice than what is expected during the independent seatwork period. Suppose further that your next assignment is to supervise the cafeteria during lunch. Again, the behaviors expected of the students and you are likely to be different from what they were in the classroom. Thus, you will need to find out the expectations for each situation or activity in which you will be working. Please note that although the expectations are likely to vary depending on the setting, the activity, and the supervisor, they will usually be consistent within those areas from day to day. Thus, once you know what is expected of students and yourself in a particular situation (e.g., on the playground, during a math test), you shouldn't need to ask your supervisor about it every time.

The "How To Do It" section of this task has general suggestions on the kind of information you need to know regarding expectations and how to get that information. In addition, Chapters 4-7 have specific suggestions for finding out about expectations related to common areas, small group work, independent seatwork, and one-on-one work with an individual student.

HOW TO DO IT:

- **For each particular job responsibility you have, find out from your immediate supervisor for that assignment what the expectations are for the students.**

If at all possible, try to meet with your immediate supervisor for each job responsibility before you actually assume the responsibility. Find out from the supervisor what the expecta-

tions for student behavior are. Specifically, you need to know what are acceptable and unacceptable student behaviors. For example, find out whether or not it's okay for students to jump off the swings on the playground. Or, whether students are permitted to ask their neighbors questions during independent seatwork. In Chapters 4, 5, 6, and 7, you will find worksheets with specifically designed questions regarding expectations for student behavior in the following situations: common areas, small group work, independent seatwork, and one-on-one work with an individual student. Again you need this information so you can monitor the students' behavior and ensure that the expectations are met.

There may be times when, as you work in a particular situation, you come to feel that a particular setting or activity would go more smoothly if the expectations for students were different. While carrying out the supervisor's expectations as given, you might want to consider asking his/her opinion about modifying the expectations. Think carefully about how to skillfully approach your supervisor with suggested changes, and be open to accepting "no" for an answer. Remember that it is the teacher's responsibility to make the decisions about the expectations for student behavior and it is your responsibility to carry out those decisions.

- **For each particular job responsibility you have, find out from your immediate supervisor for that assignment what the expectations are for you.**

When you meet with your immediate supervisor to find out about the expectations for students, you also need to ask about the expectations for you. For example, you might say something like, "Mr. Benson, before I start working in your class, I would like to find out what you want me to be doing. May I ask you some questions about how I can be of assistance?" Then ask questions about what your specific responsibilities will be and how you are expected to fulfill those responsibilities.

For example, once you have learned what the

specific expectations for student behavior are, you should find out from your supervisor what responsibility you have in communicating those expectations to the students. Will the classroom teacher actually teach the expectations and you will be responsible for reviewing them with students? Or, will you be expected to present and demonstrate the expectations to students? Whatever your level of responsibility, also ask your supervisor exactly how he or she wants you to teach/review the expectations.

NOTE: Suggestions on how to teach expectations are presented in Chapter 5 (Working with Small Groups) because this is the situation in which you are most likely to be expected to do so. As you review the suggestions in that chapter, remember that in practice you need to follow the instructions of your supervisor(s) with regard to communicating expectations.

You will also need to find out from your supervisor how you are expected to do things like monitor student behavior, reinforce responsible student behavior, and respond to student misbehavior. Tasks 3, 4, and 5 of this chapter provide general suggestions on these topics, and Chapters 4-7 include specific suggestions about how to do them when supervising common areas, working with a small group, supervising independent seatwork, and working one-on-one with an individual student. Again, the information we present is offered as suggestions only. In all situations, you need to do things the way your supervisor wants you to do them. If your supervisor tells you to do something different than what we suggest in this or any other chapter, follow your supervisor's instructions.

Figure 3.3 is a list of the general types of questions you will want to cover with your supervisor(s) regarding the expectations for your behavior. Reproducible worksheets in Chapters 4-7 include specifically tailored questions regarding the expectations for student behavior and the expectations for you in the particular situations covered in those chapters.

Once you have found out from your immediate supervisor for a particular job responsibility what is expected of the students and you, invite your supervisor to give you feedback on how you are doing your job. For example, you might say something like, "Thank you. I think I understand what is expected, but please let me know if there is anything you want me to do differently. I want to be as helpful as I possibly can in carrying out your expectations." If your supervisor is someone who has had no formal training in being a supervisor and/or someone who might be hesitant to correct you, reassuring him or her that you welcome input may increase the chances that you will get the kind of immediate and direct information that will help you be more successful in your job.

Figure 3.3

GENERAL QUESTIONS REGARDING EXPECTATIONS

Communicating expectations to students

• Should I teach students the behavioral expectations or have they already been taught what is expected of them?

• If students have already been taught the expectations, should I review them?

• If I am to teach or review expectations, how much time should I spend and what methods should I use?

Monitoring student behavior

• Am I the only adult monitoring this activity?

• What method(s) should I use to monitor the students?

• What specific behaviors/situations am I supposed to monitor?

• What situations/events, if any, should I be prepared for or especially vigilant about?

Reinforcing responsible student behavior

• Are there particular behaviors or expectations that I should try to notice and praise?

• Are there ways of providing praise (positive feedback) that these students are particularly responsive to? that they are particularly unresponsive to?

Responding to (correcting) student misbehavior

• If a student misbehaves, how should I respond? (NOTE: You may wish to ask this as a series of "What if a student _____ ?" questions.)

• Are there particular correction strategies that I should use with specific misbehaviors?

• Are there any particular correction strategies that I should avoid using?

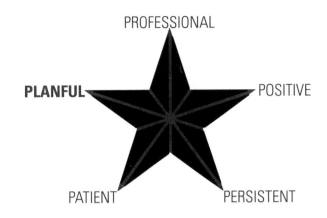

PROFESSIONAL

PLANFUL ◄ ► POSITIVE

PATIENT PERSISTENT

TASK 3:

Actively monitor student behavior.

*W*henever you are working with students, you need to monitor their behavior in some fashion. This is important for a couple of reasons. First, monitoring is the only way for you to know whether students are meeting behavioral expectations-which is necessary for making effective decisions about the kind of information/responses you will give to students regarding their behavior. (Tasks 4 and 5 address how to provide positive feedback and respond to misbehavior.) Second, monitoring student behavior gives you an opportunity to prevent potentially dangerous or problematic situations before they occur. We have highlighted the "Planful" point of the five-point star for this task, because you will be more successful if you think ahead of time about how you will monitor student behavior in various situations.

The most useful and efficient techniques for monitoring student behavior are: a) to physically circulate throughout the setting in which you are working; and b) to visually scan the setting in which you are working on a continuous basis. Systematic scanning and circulating become more important the more students you have to monitor and the bigger the physical space involved. Circulating has an added benefit in terms of managing student behavior because your physical presence itself tends to reduce student misbehavior. It's human nature. Just as most drivers are more likely to adhere to the speed limit when a police officer is present, so too are students more likely to follow behavioral expectations when you are physically close to them.

The "How To Do It" section of this task contains specific suggestions on the strategies of circulating and scanning.

HOW TO DO IT:

• **Circulate, or move about, among the students with whom you are working and/or whom you are supervising.**

Circulating means moving continually and unpredictably among the students. It is an especially important strategy when you are supervising common areas (e.g., cafeteria, playground, etc.), independent work periods, or cooperative group activities.

Circulating allows you to be near the students—which not only means that you can communicate your concern for and interest in them, but also lets the students know that should someone choose to engage in something other than the expected behaviors, you will be likely to notice. The most obvious things you will do as you move among the students are prevent accidents/problems and respond to (correct) students who are misbehaving. However, be sure to use the opportunity to encourage responsible behavior by interacting positively with students (e.g., smile at them, say "hi" and address them by name), helping students who need help, answering student questions, and giving positive feedback to students who are meeting expectations.

When you are circulating, the idea is to keep moving. That is, you want to avoid spending the majority of your time in any one place and you want to avoid moving in predictable ways so that students can't determine if/when you won't be near them for a significant amount of time. If students figure out that no one ever

checks in the boys' restroom except during the last five minutes of recess, misbehavior is likely to occur in that restroom during the first 10 minutes of recess. Always keep in mind the specific setting you are in, and be intentional about where you go and how long you stay (e.g., some spots in the cafeteria may tend to have more problems than others).

When more than one person will be supervising a setting (especially a large common area such as the playground or cafeteria), coordinate who will be responsible for which specific areas. For example, on the playground one person might circulate throughout the blacktop and equipment area, while the other person circulates throughout the grassy area where students play soccer and football.

Circulating can be more difficult to do when your primary assignment is working with a small group or one-on-one with an individual student, and you have other students to supervise at the same time. However, you can build in ways to move about periodically. For example, if you are doing 30 minutes of reading practice with a small group, you might give the students in the group a short task to perform indepen-

dently half-way through the 30-minute period. Use that time to quickly circulate among the other students, then return and resume working with the group.

- **As much as possible, visually scan the setting in which you are working on a continuous basis.**

Regardless of whatever else you are doing, frequently and intentionally look around at the students and the area over which you have direct responsibility. For example, when you are supervising a large common area, you should visually sweep across the entire area you are responsible for. Occasionally glance at the areas supervised by other adults just to see if anyone needs your assistance. When you are circulating, don't just look at the students nearest to you—visually sweep every place students might be—even a learning center across the room. When you are working with an individual student, occasionally stand up and look around the room. When you are working with a small group, periodically look up from the group and find out what is going on with other students. If you are working with a larger group, make a point of visually scanning the back rows and the front corners. Don't wait for misbehavior before you look up.

As with circulating, while you are scanning, you want to be looking for any misbehaviors that require correction. If a student is engaged in a misbehavior, go to the student and implement an appropriate correction procedure (more information on this will be presented in Task 5). And, as with circulating, always look for opportunities to acknowledge and encourage responsible behavior. For example, as you scan, if you notice that a particular student who often tends to be off-task is working, go to that student at the next opportunity and give him or her age-appropriate positive feedback. Or, if you see students on the playground who are dealing with a conflict in a responsible way, go to the group and congratulate them on the maturity with which they are handling the situation.

Finally, use visual scanning to identify students who may have questions or otherwise need your assistance. Remember, you are not just scanning for responsible and irresponsible behaviors, but also to determine whether you can provide help or otherwise be a resource to students. If you notice a student on the playground who appears somewhat lost, go to that student and help him get involved in a game with other students. During independent work periods, look for students who have signaled that they need assistance.

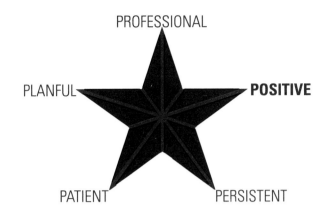

PROFESSIONAL

PLANFUL — POSITIVE

PATIENT PERSISTENT

TASK 4:

Reinforce responsible student behavior.

One of the most important tools you have for managing students' behavior is to reinforce their responsible behavior. Reinforcing responsible behavior is providing a pleasant consequence after the behavior that results in that behavior occurring more often in the future (see Figure 3.1 in Task 1, page 58). To use this tool, you need to "catch" a student, or students, in the act of behaving in a responsible manner and then do something that will be meaningful to the student(s) so that the student(s) will want to behave in that same responsible manner in the future.

In general, the easiest thing you can do is provide positive feedback when students behave in responsible, productive ways. You can give this positive feedback non-verbally (e.g., smiling, winking, etc.) or as verbal or written praise. It's important to realize, however, that poorly implemented positive feedback can be ineffective or even detrimental. For example, if verbal praise embarrasses a student, instead of increasing the probability that the student will behave responsibly in the future, it is more likely that the student will behave irresponsibly in order to reduce the chances of being embarrassed again.

There are other means of reinforcing responsible behavior that tend to be a bit more complicated. They involve such things as tangible rewards (e.g., food) and/or structured point systems. The decision about whether or not to use these kinds of reinforcers needs to be made by your supervisor. However, you should be aware that they also need to be implemented well or they can be ineffective or counterproductive.

The "How To Do It" section of this chapter contains guidelines for giving effective positive feedback, as well as some general suggestions on how to effectively use more complicated reinforcers if your supervisor has decided it would be appropriate to do so.

HOW TO DO IT:

- **Always watch for and take advantage of opportunities to give students positive feedback when they are behaving responsibly.**

- **Make sure that when you give students positive feedback, it is effective.**

It's important to make sure that when you give feedback, it will increase the chances that the student will behave responsibly in the future. Following are some guidelines for providing effective positive feedback.

*—The feedback needs to be **accurate**.*

Effective positive feedback relates to a behavior or set of behaviors that did, in fact, occur. If a student receives positive feedback about something he or she did not really do, the feedback is basically meaningless (and your credibility with the student may be diminished). Therefore, if you tell a student that his accuracy on his math assignments is improving, you need to be sure that the accuracy really is improving. Similarly, you don't want to congratulate a student for demonstrating improved self-control by staying in her seat for an entire instructional period, unless she actually did stay in her seat for that whole time.

—The feedback needs to be specific and descriptive.

Effective positive feedback lets the student know exactly what it was she did that was important or useful. That is, it is information-laden. For example, when you write a positive note about a student's paper, identify the specific things she did that contributed to the quality of the paper. Writing nothing more than "Excellent Paper" at the top of a paper does not give the student any information about what aspects of the paper led to your positive reaction—for example, was it the effective use of figurative language? the organization? the choice of vocabulary? the creative use of the overall ideas? the use of topic sentences? the clarity of the descriptive language?

The following common positive feedback mistakes can be avoided by providing specific descriptions of student behavior.

The "Good Job" syndrome. It's easy to fall into a simple repetitive phrase that you use over and over and over, to give positive feedback. There are two problems with this. First, most simple phrases (e.g., "good job," "nice work," "yes," or "fantastic") do not provide specific information about what exactly the student did that was useful or important. Second, when a phrase is overused, it becomes like background noise, and students will cease to "hear" it.

Making judgments or drawing conclusions about the student. Be very cautious about stating, or implying, that a student is "good" or "smart" or "wonderful." For example, if a student answers a difficult question, it can be tempting to say something like, "Allison, you are so smart." However, a statement like this not only doesn't provide specific information about what the student did, but it may imply to the student that if she had not come up with that particular answer, you might not think of her as smart. It's far more effective to say, "Allison, you applied the formula, performed a series of computations, and came up with the correct answer."

Calling attention to yourself. A fairly common way to praise is to say something like, "I like the way you . . . ." Even when what follows specifically describes the behavior, that initial phrase may inadvertently be taken by students to mean that they should behave to "please" you. In fact, your ultimate goal is for students to behave responsibly because it helps them be successful learners. Another problem with an "I like the way you . . . ." statement is that some students might get the idea that you "like" them when they are good, which in turn could imply you don't like them when they are not good. Keep the focus of your feedback on the students and what they have done, not on your likes and dislikes. The one exception to this is when a student does something particularly helpful for you. In that case, it's fine to let the student know that you appreciate his/her help. For example, if you drop some papers and a student helps you pick them up, it is reasonable and logical to say something like, "Thank you for helping me pick those papers up. I appreciate working with such a thoughtful student."

—*The feedback needs to be **contingent**.*

Positive feedback is far more effective when it is given for behavior that has some level of importance. If the behavior is something that is overly simple for the individual who demonstrated it, the praise may be insulting rather than reinforcing. For example, imagine that someone you know and respect (e.g., your minister or your boss) watches you drive into a parking lot and park. As you step out of your car, this person comes over to you and says, "That was an excellent left turn into this parking lot! You used your turn signals, checked your blind spot, and controlled your speed as you pulled into the parking space so that you didn't scratch the cars on either side of you." Now, this feedback may be

accurate and specific and descriptive, but it is also likely to be meaningless (at best) and/or insulting (at worst) to you. It implies that these driving behaviors are something special, when to an experienced driver making a left turn into a parking lot and successfully getting into a parking space are really no big deal. You would probably wonder why the person was being so gushy and excited. It's even possible that receiving this meaningless (or insulting) feedback would reduce your respect for that person.

There are three major circumstances under which positive feedback is contingent. The first is when the feedback occurs while someone is learning a new skill or behavior. For example, if you had a good teacher when you were first learning to drive, that person may have given you positive feedback similar to the statements in the parking lot example. However, at a time when you may have only driven once or twice before, those statements would have provided

specific and descriptive confirmation of what you did correctly, and they probably would not have been at all insulting or meaningless.

The second circumstance under which feedback is contingent is when it concerns a behavior that requires effort—whether or not the behavior is new. For example, if you make a concerted effort to increase your helpfulness around the house and your partner expresses gratitude for the extra help and/or appreciation that the household chores are being more equally divided, that positive feedback would likely be very meaningful and not at all insulting to you. The behavior isn't new or particularly difficult (after all, putting socks in the hamper is not exactly rocket science), but it does take effort to change a bad habit. Positive feedback that recognizes true effort is likely to be valued by the person receiving it, and therefore likely to result in the behavior occurring more frequently in the future.

The third circumstance under which positive feedback is contingent is when the feedback relates to a behavior (or set of behaviors) about which the individual is proud. For example, think about a time when you handed in a paper on which you felt you had done an especially good job. Chances are that when you got the paper back, you looked at the score, and then went through the paper page by page to see if the instructor had written any comments. For most people, any positive comments received in these circumstances would not be viewed as meaningless or insulting. In fact, it is quite likely that you would have been pleased by the comments, particularly if the instructor described which parts of the paper were well thought out or well written.

—*The feedback needs to be **age appropriate**.*

The way you give positive feedback to a kindergarten student will be different from the way you give it to a high school student. With younger students, you can basically do anything because they're appreciative and easy to please. With older students, on the other hand, you'll want to use more sophisticated vocabulary to describe the behavior and to focus on more advanced behaviors. At the same time, it's especially critical with older students not to embarrass them when providing positive feedback. Middle school students in particular generally feel a great deal of peer pressure to fit in and be "cool" (or whatever the current word for "cool" happens to be). These students tend to get thousands of messages that suggest that being good is "geeky." Therefore, if you provide positive feedback that in any way embarrasses a student, not only won't it be reinforcing, but it may actually discourage the student from behaving responsibly in the future. Many students, for example, will start to behave irresponsibly if they are praised in a way that gets them accused of being a "teacher's pet." If you find that students seem to be embarrassed when you give positive feedback, you might consider experimenting with one or more of the following suggestions:

Use a quiet voice. If students feel you are making a public display of them, they are more likely to feel embarrassed in front of their friends.

Be brief. If you go on and on, it makes it more difficult for the student to accept the praise graciously.

Be somewhat businesslike. If you sound too excited or pleased when you provide praise, the student may feel like, "I pleased this adult—goody goody." You're better off simply stating the positive behavior(s) the student exhibited.

Avoid pausing and looking at the student after you praise. A pause can imply to the student that you expect her to respond, which can put her in a difficult position (Should I smile? Should I say thank you?). For many students, especially one who has an image of being "tough," smiling at or thanking an adult in front of peers can be socially embarrassing. A student like this is more likely to make a smart aleck comment or misbehave just to reassert to peers how tough and bad she is.

Praise more than one student. As a general rule, if you praise at least three students, it takes pressure off each individual student.

—The feedback needs to be given in a manner that is comfortable to you.

The preceding guidelines may make it seem like there is one right way to give positive feedback. Nothing could be further from the truth. There is plenty of room for individual style, even when you incorporate our recommendations. If you have a businesslike personality you can, and should, employ a more businesslike style of providing positive feedback. If you tend to be excited and energetic, you may be somewhat more "cheerleader-like" when giving feedback. A soft-spoken person's feedback will probably be more soft-spoken than that of someone more boisterous. In most cases, the more comfortable you are giving feedback, the more comfortable your students will be receiving it. In fact, you really only need to think about making adjustments if your students are not responding well to your current style of positive feedback.

- **If you use tangible rewards or some kind of structured point system, implement it as effectively as possible.**

Remember, the decision about whether to reinforce responsible behavior with tangible rewards (such as food) or some kind of structured point system must come from your supervisor. Do not make this decision on your own. Furthermore, if your supervisor does want you to use tangible rewards or a structured point system, you need to follow his/her instructions for implementation. However, you may wish to consider the following tips:

—Continue to provide effective positive feedback.

Using tangible rewards or structured point systems does not reduce the importance of providing positive feedback to students. In fact, it's a good idea to make a positive comment about the student's behavior before you give a reward or point. These comments should follow the guidelines for effective positive feedback in terms of being accurate, contingent, and so on.

—When you use a point system, keep your energy and enthusiasm for the system high.

You will be the fuel that keeps any system run-

77

ning. If you don't "fill 'er up" with your excitement, interest, and support, the students are very likely to lose interest even if the rewards they are working toward are compelling.

—Keep your focus on the students' behavior rather than the rewards they earn.

—Concentrate your energy and excitement on "Look at what you did!" rather than "Look at what you get."

When you keep your focus on the students' improved growth, maturity, progress, and so on, you increase the chances that the students will begin to work less for the "rewards" and more for their sense of satisfaction in meeting expectations successfully.

—When using tangible rewards, gradually increase the amount of positive behavior required to get the reward.

The idea is to eventually eliminate the tangible reward and have the responsible behavior itself be the "reward." For example, say you're using tangible rewards when working with a small group of low-functioning first graders. You might start by giving the students a piece of cereal every time they respond correctly. As student performance improves, you should plan on giving the reward after every two or three correct responses. Again, your immediate supervisor should help you make these judgments.

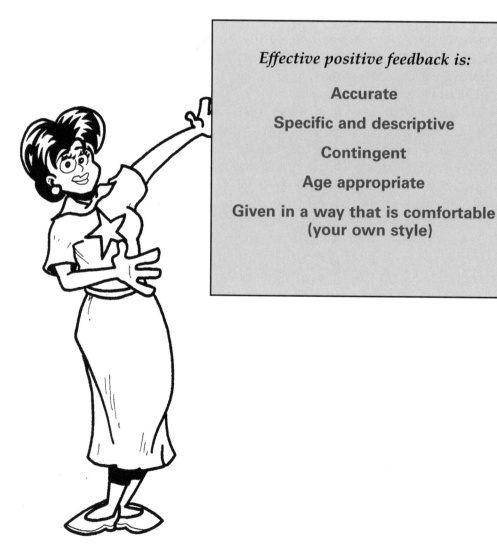

Effective positive feedback is:

Accurate

Specific and descriptive

Contingent

Age appropriate

Given in a way that is comfortable (your own style)

PROFESSIONAL

PLANFUL   POSITIVE

PATIENT   PERSISTENT

TASK 5:

Respond to irresponsible student behavior in ways that will help the students learn to behave more responsibly.

In your role as a paraeducator, there will undoubtedly be times when you will have to respond to (i.e., correct) irresponsible student behavior. Effective responses help reduce the probability that the student(s) will exhibit the irresponsible behavior in the future. Furthermore, when you can identify why the student is misbehaving, then you can tailor your response to help the student(s) learn to exhibit more productive behavior the next time similar circumstances occur. As you read through the information in this task, remember that these are suggestions only. Your actual responses to student misbehavior will be determined by your supervisor.

Responding effectively to misbehavior involves all five points of the star. That is, you

need to respond with professionalism—avoiding doing or saying anything you might later regret. You also need to be planful about how you will respond to misbehavior—trying to decide what to do about misbehavior RIGHT NOW almost always results in being less effective than if you had considered in advance, How will I handle it if a student . . . .?

Patience is essential because responding to student misbehavior with emotion can inadvertently reinforce the misbehavior. Some students like nothing better than to get adults flustered, angry or frustrated. Being patient and calm with students when you respond to misbehavior not only decreases the possibility the misbehavior will be reinforced, but also increases the likelihood that the student(s) will learn to behave responsibly. In addition, staying calm and being patient decreases the chances that you might say or do something in the "heat of the moment" that you may later regret.

Persistence is necessary to be consistent, and consistency is essential because your responses to misbehavior should, quite literally, be predictable and boring (or they may end up being reinforcing). For example, a student who misbehaves on Monday and "gets away with it," then receives a correction for the same misbehavior on Tuesday, will just about have to try exhibiting the behavior again on Wednesday to find out what will happen. Persistence means, in part, that you "never give up." You respond to (correct) the misbehavior as often as necessary. Learning to respond to misbehavior with patience and persistence is one of the toughest jobs for anyone working with children.

Being positive with regard to misbehavior does not mean that you respond by praising students who misbehave. Rather it means that you understand how important it is to be positive with students when they are not engaged in misbehavior. Your corrections are more likely to change student misbehavior if you are also interacting with students in friendly and positive ways when they are behaving responsibly.

NOTE: How to deal with especially difficult behavior is covered in Task 7 of this chapter, "Prevent (and/or deal effectively with) student non-compliance."

HOW TO DO IT:

• Be professional when responding to student misbehavior.

Student misbehavior can be frustrating and upsetting; however, you need to be careful not to do or say anything that you might regret later. Never get into physical or verbal confrontations with students. Never call a student a name. (These may seem unnecessary to even bring up, but some students are very skilled at "getting under the skin" of adults in positions of authority.) We have three major tips to share on how to maintain your professionalism when dealing with misbehavior.

—Don't take it personally.

When a student misbehaves, he or she is probably not thinking about doing something to you. The student would likely misbehave with anyone who was in a position of authority. So, whether a student insults you, tries to argue with you, or even accuses you of being unfair or unreasonable, keep reminding yourself not to take it personally.

—*Give yourself time to think before you respond.*

When confronting tense situations with students, there can be a tendency to want to respond quickly. Counting slowly to three or taking a couple of slow deep breaths will give you time to make sure that your response will be professional-not something you will later regret having done or said.

—*View misbehavior as an opportunity to teach.*

Remind yourself that any time a student misbehaves, you have a chance to teach that student a more productive way of behaving. This can take your focus off the misbehavior and turn it toward considering what you as a "professional" can do to help the student.

- ## Be planful about your responses to student misbehavior.

The more prepared you are to deal with student misbehavior, the more likely it is that your efforts to correct (reduce/eliminate) the behavior will be effective. Check with your immediate supervisor(s) about specifically how you should respond to various misbehaviors in each setting. If you have worked or are working in a particular setting, you might think about the student misbehaviors you have observed in that setting, and tailor your questions—for example, "What do you want me to do if a student . . . .?" Following are some general procedures for responding to misbehavior based on the reason for and/or type of the behavior. You might want to discuss these with your supervisor. Remember, in Chapters 4-7 you will find examples of correction procedures specifically for misbehaviors that are likely to occur in common areas, during small group work, during independent work periods, and when working with an individual student.

—*If the student is unable to behave responsibly, adjust the expectation.*

If a student has a physical or neurological disability that makes it impossible for him/her to meet the expectation, modify the expectation rather than try to change the student's behavior.

—*If the student does not know how to behave responsibly, teach the responsible behavior.*

When a student has sufficient language skills, you can actually tell the student how to exhibit the responsible behavior. If the student is very young (preschool to first grade) or has low language skills, you can use modeling, redirection, and/or imagery. Modeling involves showing the student the responsible behavior. Redirection means to physically help the student exhibit the responsible behavior (e.g., gently escorting a kindergarten student who is wandering around, back to his seat). Imagery means to give students a mental picture that is familiar to them (e.g., zip your mouth; hands and feet inside like a turtle).

—*If a student seems to be seeking attention with the misbehavior, respond with planned ignoring IF YOU CAN.*

Actually, the most important correction for misbehavior that stems from a student's need for attention is to provide lots of attention when the student is behaving responsibly. When the misbehavior does occur, and it's possible to do so, ignore it. For example, if a student repeatedly calls out to you to help her instead of raising her hand and waiting patiently, consciously ignore the calling out AND respond immediately when the student raises her hand or exhibits some other responsible behavior (e.g., working on the task). Keep in mind that when you ignore a behavior designed to get attention, the behavior is likely to get worse before it gets better.

—*If it is the first or second time a (minor) misbehavior has occurred, respond by providing information on the expectations.*

For infrequent and minor misbehavior, the easiest and most effective correction often is to say something like, "The expectation is . . . ."

—*If it is a major and/or chronic misbehavior, respond by calmly and consistently implementing specific corrective consequences (e.g., assigning time-owed).*

Ask your supervisor about corrective consequences you should use and/or review Chapters 4-7 for ideas appropriate to the specific situations covered in those chapters. Responding calmly and consistently with chronic offenders is a real skill. Using "practiced one-liners," or canned responses, that you repeat unemotionally and in a broken-record fashion will give students information and help you not to get involved in power struggles.

NOTE: There may be times when your supervisor asks you to collect information on particular misbehaviors. This is not just busy work. The information will be used to determine whether the current responses or correction procedures are resulting in a reduction in the misbehavior, no change in the misbehavior, or (unfortunately, this does sometimes happen) an increase in the misbehavior. Task 6 in this chapter has more information on collecting and summarizing objective information on student behaviors.

• Be patient when responding to student misbehavior.

No matter what your response to a misbehavior is—ignoring, giving a verbal reprimand, assigning time-out—implement it calmly. Avoid showing tension (e.g., clenched jaw, hands shaking or held as fists). Use a matter-of-fact tone of voice, and speak at your normal rate of speech or even a little bit more slowly. Try to present a supportive rather than a confrontational (fighting) stance or posture.

If a student's misbehavior really makes you angry, take a few deep breaths to relax before you respond. Keep in mind that for some students, an angry or hostile response from adults is the biggest "payoff" they can receive. In those cases, getting angry is the last thing in the world you want to do—because it will just serve to increase the chances the student will exhibit the same misbehavior in the future. If, as may happen despite your best efforts, a student does "get to you," learn from the situation. Tell yourself that even though the student was able to "push your buttons" this time, the next time you will stay calm. Mentally rehearse the situation and

envision yourself responding calmly rather than emotionally. "Next time Robert's actions are upsetting me, I will stay relaxed and simply inform him of the consequence." It is okay to make a mistake when responding to student misbehavior; just don't keep making the same mistake over and over.

• Be persistent when responding to misbehavior.

Don't expect miracle cures when dealing with students who exhibit chronic misbehavior. It is unrealistic to think that you can effectively respond to a chronic misbehavior one or two times and then the misbehavior will never happen again. In most cases, you will have to correct and correct and correct. The phrase "managing student behavior" conveys the ongoing nature of the process. It means that each time a misbehavior occurs, you need to respond calmly and consistently. Thus, if you decide that a particular misbehavior should be corrected by assigning time-owed, you need to assign time-owed every time the misbehavior occurs.

Be especially careful not to be lenient on days that you feel particularly calm, happy, or tired. When you are feeling good, a misbehavior that you usually correct may not annoy you and so you may think, "Oh, I won't bother to correct that behavior today—it isn't really that bad." When you are tired, it can be tempting to think, "I just don't have the energy to deal with this. I'm going to ignore it." In both cases, not responding is being inconsistent. Whether or not it seems so at that moment, you need to consistently follow through with your correction procedures.

You may get discouraged about the number of times you have to keep correcting a particular misbehavior. If you start feeling frustrated and begin thinking, "How many times am I going to have to deal with this misbehavior?" answer yourself by saying, "As many times as it takes." That really is the meaning of persistence—responding to (correcting) misbehavior as many times as it takes for the behavior to begin to improve.

• Be "positive" when the student is not engaged in misbehavior. (Develop a 3 to 1 ratio of positive to negative interactions.)

At first glance this may sound a little odd, but the time when you have the most influence in correcting a student's misbehavior is the time between misbehaviors—that is, when the student is not engaged in the misbehavior. This is when you can give the student attention for and information about her responsible behavior.

Some students may not know exactly how to behave responsibly. If you can catch them behaving responsibly—and comment on their responsibility and describe exactly what they are doing—you help them learn the details of behaving in a responsible manner.

Other students are so starved for attention, they misbehave because it's how they can gain the most adult attention in the easiest manner possible. If you pay attention to every student more frequently when the student is making responsible choices, you demonstrate that it is easier to get attention and recognition with responsible behavior than with misbehavior.

Your goal should be to interact with every student at least three times when the student is behaving responsibly for every one time that you have to interact with the student regarding misbehavior. The three "positive" interactions can not only include giving the student positive feedback (see Task 4), but also things like greeting the student as she enters the room, asking the student how her day is going, and/or finding out whether the student has any questions or needs any help. All of these interactions demonstrate to the student that you notice her and value her, and that she does not need to misbehave to get attention.

PROFESSIONAL

PLANFUL   POSITIVE

PATIENT   PERSISTENT

TASK 6:

Understand some basic concepts related to information-based decision-making.

Information-based decision-making in schools means that decisions about such things as a student's instructional placement, the instructional materials or curricula used for instruction, or components in a Behavior Improvement Plan will be based on objective information or "data" rather than on "gut instinct." To understand why this is so important, think about going to a physician because you have been experiencing abdominal pain. You are not likely to be comfortable with a physician who notes the reason for your visit, takes one look at you as you walk in the door, and says, "I think you need a kidney transplant. When can we schedule the surgery?" A good physician will use objective information—from her physical examination of you and from any lab work that is done—along with your self-reports, to determine a course of treatment. In addition, a good physician will collect more objective information
after the treatment to determine whether it has helped or not.

In Chapter 2, we suggested that effective communication includes objectively reporting what you see and hear. This was an introduction to the idea of objective information. Objective information is information that is specific and measurable. Consider the following statements, "Jevonne is failing history because he has turned in only 32% of his homework assignments. However, on the assignments he has turned in, he has averaged 91% correct." These statements are accurate accounts of Jevonne's actual performance. Now consider the statement, "Jevonne is really smart, but lazy." At first glance, "smart but lazy" may seem to be a pretty good summary of objective information showing 91% accuracy, but only 32% completion. However, the real reason Jevonne is having trouble with work completion is that he works every day after school until midnight to provide financial support for his family. Objective information is more accurate and therefore more useful than subjective opinions for making decisions about students.

Paraeducators are often asked to collect information on a student. Sometimes the information is used to help staff make decisions about a particular student's behavior. In special education, the information collected is often used to help the special education teacher (or the student's case worker) determine whether the student is making progress toward the behavioral and/or academic goals specified on the IEP. Whatever the reason, the information needs to be collected/recorded systematically and summarized in a usable manner.

For example, suppose a teacher was concerned about Felicia's swearing. The teacher might ask the paraeducator to collect objective information on Felicia's behavior. The paraeducator would carefully note each of Felicia's swearing incidents on a recording form every day for two weeks. The information would then be summarized on a chart so that Felicia's teacher could easily determine whether implementing an intensive Behavior Improvement Plan would be necessary to help Felicia reduce her swearing. If the paraeducator were only to collect information on Felicia's classroom swearing for one day in the two week period, there might not be enough information to determine the extent of the problem or the day may not represent a typical day in terms of that behavior. Furthermore, if the paraeducator were to haphazardly write the information on little slips of paper, some of which end up at home, some at her desk, and some in a notebook, rather than record it systematically and summarize it on a chart, it would be harder (if not impossible) for the teacher to get a clear picture of the situation.

The "How To Do It" section of this task includes brief explanations of five major types of information that are commonly collected in schools, along with some basic suggestions on how to collect and record that information. Our purpose in presenting this material is to help you become familiar with what you might be asked to do. If you are, in fact, asked to collect information as part of your job responsibilities, be sure to find out from the supervisor making the request what type of information you are

expected to collect, how you are to collect that information, and how you are to summarize or report the information.

HOW TO DO IT:

• Understand the concept of "baseline" information.

Information that is collected before any attempt has been made to address a problem behavior is called baseline information. This information is used for several purposes. First of all, it helps school staff determine whether or not the problem is severe enough to require intervention. For example, if the information collected on Felicia's swearing indicated that she swore an average of two times in a week, her teacher might decide that an intensive Behavior Improvement Plan wasn't needed. When an intervention is deemed necessary, the baseline information becomes the point of comparison for determining intervention effectiveness.

In Felicia's case, for example, the actual baseline information showed that Felicia was swearing an average of 35 times a day. This clearly indicated a problem, so her teacher decided to implement a Behavior Improvement Plan (BIP). She asked the paraeducator to continue collecting information on Felicia's swearing incidents. After the BIP had been in place for approximately two weeks, the teacher reviewed the information on Felicia's swearing. The information indicated that the number of swearing incidents was going down, so the teacher decided that the plan was effective and continued implementing it. Now, if the number of swearing incidents had been staying about the same or was going up, that would have suggested that the plan was not effective. The teacher would have then had to decide whether to modify the plan being used or develop a new plan. To summarize, baseline information is the information collected before a change or intervention is begun.

• Be somewhat familiar with the five major types of information (data) that you may be asked to collect.

For any particular student or situation, one or two types of information will usually be collected. (Collecting more than one type of information allows you to "confirm" the findings and to get a richer picture of the situation.) Following are descriptions of the five most common types of information collected in schools. This summary has been adapted, with permission, from a very useful program of interventions entitled Project RIDE, which is published by Sopris West.

• **Frequency information has to do with the number of times the target behavior (i.e., the behavior of concern) occurs during a specific time period (session).**

EXAMPLES:

Out-of-seat behavior might be expressed as the number of times a student gets out of his seat in an hour. Oral reading fluency is often expressed as the number of words a student reads correctly in a minute.

Frequency information is collected by recording each occurrence of the target behavior within the specified time. This can be done using one of the following recording techniques:

• A tally sheet on a clipboard or an index card in your pocket.

Figure 3.4 Frequency Graph

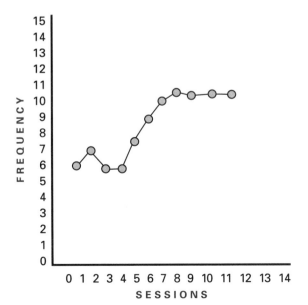

Each time the target behavior occurs, you make a mark on a sheet or a card. You then total the tally marks at the end of the specified period. If you are collecting information on several different behaviors for one student, you can divide the sheet or card into sections. If you are collecting information on several students, you might use a different colored sheet or card for each student. For example, you may have a yellow card on which you have written "Jan: Out-of-Seat" and a green card with a line down the middle on which you have written "Joshua: Out-of-Seat" and "Joshua: Negative Comments."

• Use a wrist or golf counter.

Each time the target behavior occurs, you advance the counter. You record the total on the counter at the end of the specified time period.

• Use paper clips in a pocket.

You keep a supply of small objects (paper clips, beads, beans, buttons) in one pocket or container. Each time the target behavior occurs, you transfer one of the objects from the first pocket or container to another pocket or a container. At the end of the specified time period, you count and record the number of objects in the second pocket or container.

Collected frequency information can be displayed on a simple chart (see Figure 3.4), which makes it easy to review and evaluate.

• **Duration information has to do with the total amount of time a student engages in the target behavior during a specific time period (session).**

EXAMPLE:

Off-task behavior may be expressed as the number of minutes a student is off task within the 50 minute class period.

Duration information is useful when a behavior occurs infrequently but lasts for long periods of time. For example, if a student was screaming continuously for 45 minutes during a class period, frequency information would not give as

Figure 3.5 Duration Graph

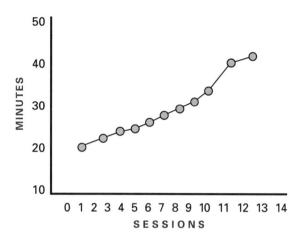

accurate a picture of the problem as duration information. To collect duration information, you need a stopwatch or sports watch. Start the watch when the target behavior (e.g., screaming) begins and stop it when the target behavior stops. Record how many minutes occurred. If the behavior happens again during the specified time, repeat the process and add the number of minutes in the subsequent incident to the original time. At the end of the specified time period, you note the total number of incidents and record the total number of minutes (e.g., the student was off-task a total of 23 minutes during the 50 minute class period).

An alternative way of recording duration is to use a tape recorder. Each time the target behavior begins, start the tape recorder recording. When the behavior ceases, stop the recording. Continue the process throughout the specified time period (e.g., class period, morning, day). At the end of the time period, record yourself saying, "STOP." Later, you can rewind the tape, then press play and start a stopwatch at the same time. Let the tape and the watch run (you can grade papers or clean the room) until you hear the word STOP. Stop the watch and make note of the total amount of time.

Duration information can be recorded on a chart such as the one shown in Figure 3.5

- **Percentage information has to do with the number of correct (and/or incorrect) responses relative to the total number of responses possible for a specific assignment or time period.**

EXAMPLE:

A student who correctly answered 25 problems on a 30-problem assignment, had a percentage correct of 83%. A student who followed directions 6 times out of 10 could be said to be compliant 60% of the time.

Percentage correct is calculated by dividing the number of correct responses by the total number of responses possible. In the preceding example, 25 (the number of correct responses) was divided by 30 (the total number of possible responses). The answer is 0.83, which can be written as 83%.

Once collected, percentage information can also be charted. When charting percentages, the vertical axis of the chart should range from 0 to one 100. See Figure 3.6 for an example.

Figure 3.6 Percentage Graph

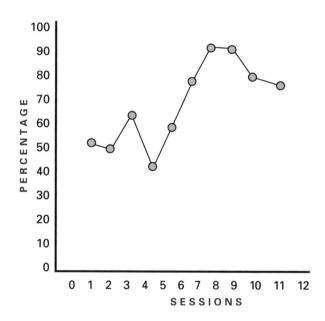

Figure 3.7 Latency Graph

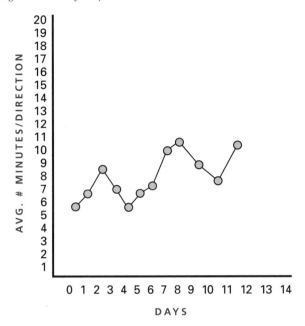

DAYS

• **Magnitude or Quality information has to do with "rating" a behavior on some kind of scale—for example, 0 to 5.**

EXAMPLE:

At the end of each class period, a teacher and a student evaluate the degree of cooperation and respect the student demonstrated toward the teacher. A rating of zero means that the student was disrespectful and uncooperative the entire time, while a rating of five represents that the student was respectful and cooperative the entire class period.

Magnitude and quality ratings information may tend to be more subjective. However, if the various points on the scale have been carefully defined and everyone understands how the ratings will be determined, ratings can be a useful form of information.

This information might be charted by marking an X each day for the teacher's rating and a • for the student's rating. See Figure 3.8 for an example.

• **Latency information has to do with how much time goes by between when a specific direction is given and when the student responds to that direction.**

(NOTE: Latency information is almost always used in the context of compliance and following directions.)

Latency information is also collected with the use of a stopwatch or sports watch. You start the watch when you give the student a direction (e.g., you tell the student to begin working). When the student begins to follow that direction, you stop the watch. You do this each time you give the student a direction throughout the specified time period. At the end of the specified time period, you can record the total number of minutes. When you divide the total number of minutes by the total number of directions given, you get the average number of minutes the student took in that time period to start following a direction after it was given. See the sample in Figure 3.7

Figure 3.8 Magnitude Graph

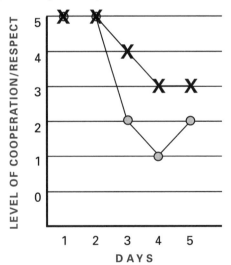

DAYS

PROFESSIONAL

PLANFUL — POSITIVE

PATIENT — **PERSISTENT**

TASK 7:

Prevent (and/or deal effectively with) student non-compliance.

*O*ne type of student misbehavior that can be particularly difficult for anyone (paraeducator, teacher, or even a principal) to handle well is non-compliance or defiance— the refusal to follow a direction. Defiance occurs when an adult asks a student to do something and the student in some way (with words or actions) communicates, "I'm not gonna, and you can't make me." Defiance may be demonstrated by a student in a variety of ways. Following are some examples:

A student is given an assignment and only partially or half-heartedly completes it.

A student is given a direction to begin working on an assignment and she sits and does nothing; she doesn't even acknowledge that she is being spoken to.

A student is running in the hall and when asked by an adult to stop, he just runs right by the adult.

A student is instructed to clean up a mess he made in the cafeteria. The student denies he made the mess and continues to argue about having to clean it up.

A student is told that he needs to redo part of an assignment. The student looks the adult in the eye and says, "I don't have to do what you tell me to do."

A student is told she needs to go to time-out because of a minor misbehavior. The student flies into a rage, screaming and kicking and knocking materials about.

Defiance may occur for a variety of reasons. Although generally it will be your supervisor's responsibility to determine exactly why an individual student is chronically non-compliant, you should be aware of some common reasons for defiance.

The direction is not clear (e.g., it's too long, uses unfamiliar terms, etc.). For example, if a student is directed to, "Get ready," it may be confusing and unclear what the student is supposed to do.

91

The student does not remember or understand exactly what is expected or does not know how to comply, because the instruction is complex or involves multiple steps. The student then becomes frustrated.

The student has learned to get her own way. In other words, through her experiences, the student has discovered that if she refuses when asked to do something, the adult will eventually back off and remove the demand.

The "How To Do It" section of this chapter starts with tips on preventing defiance by making sure that you give directions effectively. It then presents information on dealing effectively with defiance if it does occur. The key to handling student non-compliance is persistence.

HOW TO DO IT:

• Lessen the probability of student non-compliance by giving effective directions.

Some adults can give a direction to a student and the student will always make an effort to follow the direction. Other adults can give the exact same direction to the exact same student and the student will be non-compliant. What is the difference? First of all, if the adult has been positive, inviting, firm, and has maintained high expectations with the student, the relationship he or she has established with that student increases the likelihood of compliance.

The second reason is a little harder to explain, but adults who get high levels of compliance just seem to communicate the "assumption of compliance." They have a manner that implies, "I know you are going to follow this direction." On the other hand, an adult who comes across as either "wimpy" or "bullying" is inadvertently communicating, "I know you probably won't do this so I am begging you" or "I am going to try to intimidate you into following my direction." Watch other adults in your school who have an easy and confident manner that just seems to invite cooperation from students, and try to interact with students using a similar style.

Third, some people are just better at giving directions than others. The following tips on giving directions will increase the chances that students will follow the directions you give. It is especially important to remember these tips when you are interacting with a student who has a tendency to be defiant.

—Use proximity management.

Stand close to the student when giving a direction. A direction given from across the room is more likely to be ignored by a student than one given within about three feet of the student.

—Get the student's attention.

Before you give a direction, use the student's name and a statement such as, "Roberta, listen to me please." When a student's attention has been directed toward you, there is a greater probability that the direction will be followed than had you given the direction with no advance notice.

—Use clear and simple language.

When you give a direction, use terms the student is likely to understand.

—Provide specific directions that result in observable actions.

A statement such as "Adam, stand right here," is a direction with an outcome that can be observed, whereas something like, "Change your attitude, young man" is not specific. Similarly, "Finish three problems," is a very specific direction, as opposed to, "Do your work," which is far too general.

—Give only one or two directions at a time.

This suggestion is especially important when giving directions to young students, students of limited English speaking ability, and students who have demonstrated difficulty in following directions in the past. Also, students who have memory or processing problems may be flustered by multiple directions.

An example of a multiple direction would be, "Thomas, look at me please. Finish the rest of the problems on this page, then put your work in the "Completed Work" basket. When you have done that, go to the library area and get a book to take back to your desk for silent reading. Read quietly until it is time for recess." It would be more effective to state the directions in two parts. You might start by saying, "Thomas, look at me please. Thank you. Finish the problems on this page and then raise your hand so I know you are finished." (That combines two directions; however, since the student is probably used to a classroom routine like raising his hand, it is a logical and relatively simple combination.) Then, when the student has finished the problems and raised his hand, you can give the next part of the directions.

When you have to give a series of directions, break them into clear parts and use terms such as, "first, next, last." For example, you might say, "Theresa, first you are going to walk to the office. Next you will give this paper to one of the adults in the office. Last you will go get on the bus."

It's always a good idea to verify student understanding of multiple or complex directions by having the student repeat back what he is going to do. Using the preceding example, you might say something like, "Tell me what you are going to do first. Tell me what you will do next. Tell me what you will do last."

—Give a direction, don't ask a question.

Some people have the tendency to ask a question when they really want/expect the student to follow a direction. If you say to a student, "Would you like to get started on your math assignment," and the student says, "No," that is not defiance. You asked a question and the student responded. A more clear directive would be to say, "Do all of the problems on page 53."

—State a direction positively.

That is, state what you want the student to do, rather than what you don't want the student to do. "Put the pencil on the desk" is a better direction than, "Don't tap that pencil."

—Provide visual prompts whenever possible.

For example, as you tell students to get out their math books, hold the math book. When you tell students to fold a paper in half, demonstrate what you mean.

—Allow a reasonable response time.

Some students need to process a direction in their minds for longer periods of time than other students. Do not immediately assume that a student is not complying. Wait five to fifteen seconds. If the student has not responded after fifteen seconds, repeat the instruction. If the student still does not respond, consider the correction procedures and strategies suggested in the next section, "Respond effectively when a student is non-compliant."

—Get on a "following directions roll."

When you think a student may be unlikely to follow a particular direction, give three directions the student is likely to carry out immediately before the direction that he may defy. In The Tough Kid Book, by Rhode, Reavis and Jenson, (1992), this is called "behavioral momentum." You get the student to follow a potentially problematic direction as part of a sequence of directions he will follow. Consider the following scenario.

Aaron enjoys working on the computer. However, when it is time to leave the computer lab, Aaron tends to cry, scream, and even throw himself onto the floor. So, just before it is time to leave the computer lab, the paraeducator supervising Aaron gives him three directions that have nothing to do with leaving. She says, "Aaron, tell me how many points you have in this game." (Direction No. 1) "Tell me which game you like best." (Direction No. 2) "Show me how you go back to the first screen." (Direction No. 3) Once Aaron complies with each of those directions, and she praises him for following directions, the paraeducator gives step-by-step directions for leaving the computer lab. She praises Aaron at each step along the way. "Aaron, show me how to exit this program. You sure know how to work these programs. Take out your disk. Thank you. Turn off the screen. You are doing a nice job of

following directions. Please push in your chair and let's go back to class. I am learning a lot about computers by watching you."

—Respond effectively when a student is non-compliant.

If a student refuses to follow a direction you give, you must respond. How you respond will depend, in part, on whether the defiance is a first-time event (i.e., the student has never done this before) or a chronic problem (i.e., one that happens repeatedly).

As stated previously, when you give a direction, wait for five to fifteen seconds. During this time, think about whether the direction was clear. If there is any possibility it was not, restate the direction clearly.

If the student still fails to carry out your request, and this is the first time that has happened, choose one of the following strategies that you think has the best chance of getting the student to follow the direction.

—Try humor.

Sometimes a funny comment can help diffuse a tense situation. If the student can laugh or see some humor in the situation, he may comply just because you did not "make a big deal" of this one-time-only poor choice that he made. Be careful to avoid sarcasm or saying anything that the student may interpret as you making fun of or ridiculing him. If you are not a particularly funny kind of person, this situation is probably not a good time to start because, if not done skillfully, humor may escalate the intensity of the problem. However, if you are funny and very sensitive to the needs of kids, humor can sometimes be very effective.

—Ask for cooperation.

If the student is someone you have a good relationship with and/or someone who usually does what you ask, you might try saying something supportive such as, "Kelly, I know you're having a rough day, but right now it is very important that you _____, and I know you can do it." You do not want to sound like you are begging the student, but it is okay to appeal to the student's better instincts and to use the good relationship you have with the student to help the student see that following the direction would be a good idea.

—*Offer the student a choice.*

Give the student an opportunity to have control over some part of the situation. For example, if the direction was for the student to complete the problems on page 57, you might ask the student whether she would like to do the assignment by herself or get help with the first five problems. Be sure to offer real choices. That is, both (or even all three) choices must be somewhat attractive. Many people think they are offering a choice, when in fact they are making a threat. "You can choose to do these problems now or you can do them at recess." While there is nothing wrong with this approach as a correction strategy, it is not really a choice and should not be considered as such. See the suggestion below.

—*Let the student know the result of not following the direction.*

Informing the student of what will happen if he does not follow the direction is best used when there already is an established corrective consequence for a particular misbehavior. For example, say you observe a student heading for the door in the cafeteria without having followed the rule about not leaving the table until excused. You tell the student to stop so you can speak to him, but the student keeps on walking. With a pre-set corrective consequence in place, you might say something like, "If you leave the cafeteria without permission, I will have to write a referral to the principal." Then, if the student keeps going, follow through. Write the referral. Be careful not to state a consequence that you cannot or will not carry out. In the heat of a tense moment it is easy to make an unreasonable threat.

—*Avoid ineffective responses to non-compliance*

Along with the preceding suggested correction procedures, there are some responses you want to avoid when a student is being non-compliant. They are:

—*Do not engage in arguing with the student.*

If a student tries to argue or negotiate his way out of a non-compliance situation, implement

Remember, clear directions

• **use simple language**

• **are statements—not questions**

• **state observable actions**

• **use Do statements, not Don't statements**

95

the "broken record" technique. Simply restate your direction or use a repetitive phrase each time the student offers a reason that he should not have to do what you say.

EXAMPLE:

"Please pick up those papers and put them in the trash."

"I don't have to."

"Please pick up those papers and put them in the trash."

"Why don't you do it?"

"Please pick up those papers and put them in the trash."

—Do not let a student get away with defiance.

Do not just ignore a student's refusal to follow a direction. If the student is allowed to get away with not following this direction, she will almost certainly test to see if she can get away with not following other directions. You have to do something. At a minimum, tell the student that she is not following directions. Be sure to get input from your supervisor on how you should respond in the future.

—Do not try to physically force the student to comply.

If a student refuses to follow your direction, do not attempt to grab, push, or otherwise try to "make" the student do what you say. If the student is defiant, and none of the preceding strategies are effective in getting the student to do what you've asked, you will need to talk to your supervisor about what to do.

—Follow up on chronic non-compliance

If a student has refused to follow your directions on several occasions, start by analyzing and trying to improve the quality and clarity of your directions. In addition, consider the following suggestions:

—Discuss the situation with your immediate supervisor.

Inform your supervisor of what has happened to this point. Be very specific about all incidents. Specify the directions the student has refused to carry out, what the student did or said, and what happened. Ask your supervisor for advice on how you should handle any future incidents.

—Keep records.

Following any incident of defiance, make some notes on the situation. Be sure to include the date, time, location, activity, the direction that was given, the student's response, your response, and any other information that may be relevant. Review your records and see whether you can identify any patterns to the student's behavior-for example, the student is more defiant in particular settings, during certain activities (transitions, academic subjects), around certain individuals (males or females, assistants or teachers), or under unique circumstances (e.g., when there is loud noise).

—Share any patterns you find with your immediate supervisor.

If you can identify any patterns, share them with your supervisor and work with your supervisor to design a plan for helping the student. A plan for chronic defiance might include structural/organizational modifications. For example, if your records indicate that the student is more likely to be defiant during a transition from one activity to another (which is true for many students who are non-compliant), your supervisor might suggest informing the student that a transition will occur two minutes before the transition itself. A plan might also include modifying the correction procedures used for refusal to follow directions, and implementing specific procedures for reinforcing the student for following directions. A plan of this type must be designed with your supervisor.

CHAPTER 3 ★ ACTIVITIES

THINK ABOUT IT

Use the following chart to evaluate your familiarity with the material presented in this chapter. When you have completed this activity, enter reminders about the tasks you wanted to reread or discuss into your planning calendar.

Figure 3.9 Reproducible Form

	The information was not applicable to my situation.	The information was familiar. I consistently implement the strategies presented.	The information was useful. I should reread this task at least once more this year.	Some of the information was new. I should reread this task within a month.	Much of the information was new. I should discuss it with my supervisor or with other paraeducators.
TASK 1: Become familiar with some basic concepts related to behavior.	0	1	2	3	4
TASK 2: Be clear about what is expected of the students and what is expected of you.	0	1	2	3	4
TASK 3: Actively monitor student behavior.	0	1	2	3	4
TASK 4: Reinforce responsible student behavior.	0	1	2	3	4
TASK 5: Respond to irresponsible student behavior in ways that will help students learn to behave more responsibly.	0	1	2	3	4
TASK 6: Understand some basic concepts related to information-based decision-making.	0	1	2	3	4
TASK 7: Prevent (and/or deal effectively with) student non-compliance.	0	1	2	3	4

(NOTE: On pages 205-210, in the back of the book, you will find a complete chart of all the tasks in the book. You may wish to summarize the information from each individual chapter on this single chart.)

TAKE ACTION

On a blank piece of paper, draw three columns. Label the first column with a "+," the second with a "-," and the third with an "0." (See Figure 3.9)

Figure 3.9

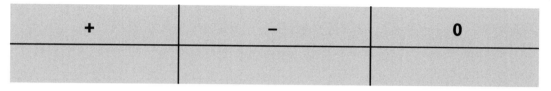

+	–	0

In the "+" column, make a list of students with whom it is easy (and even automatic) for you to maintain a 3 to 1 ratio of positive to negative interactions. In the "-" column, make a list of students whom you find yourself correcting more than interacting positively with-for example, students who may not be easy to like and/or students who are skilled at getting attention with their misbehavior. In the "0" column, list students with whom you have daily contact, but rarely (if ever) interact with.

Review your completed the chart. Congratulate yourself for the skill and professionalism you demonstrate in your interactions with students in the "+" column. Next, set specific goals for increasing the number of positive interactions you have with each of the students listed in the "-" and the "0" columns. Remember that positive interactions with you will not only help those students feel valued, but will also improve their behavior and motivation.

DISCUSS IT

Arrange with a group of colleagues to read Chapter 3 and do the Take Action activity for this chapter. Then schedule a meeting at which the group can discuss the following topics/questions.

1. Discuss the following questions/issues about how adults behave to develop your understanding of how behavior is learned and maintained. Apply this knowledge to the behavior of the students with whom you work.

   a. Do you always follow the rules when you drive a car? If not, which rules do you personally tend to be the most lax about—speed limits, parking meters, rolling stops, etc.? Why aren't you perfect in following the rules? What would get you to be more consistent in following the rules—better supervision (i.e., police more visible, but consequences at current levels) or harsher consequences (police no more visible, but fines quadrupled in amount)?

   b. What are the positive reinforcers for coming to work each day? (NOTE: At the end of some days, this list can be difficult to generate!) Be sure to include less tangible things than just the paycheck (e.g., the satisfaction of seeing a "Now I understand look" on a student's face).

   c. Describe a time/situation in which an adult or a student in the school gave you positive feedback. After each person has shared their experience, discuss how the various examples relate to/reflect the suggestions for effective feedback presented in Task 4: Reinforce responsible student behavior.

   d. Think about a time/situation in which you were given unskillful corrective feedback. It might have been from a teacher or parent when you were a child, or from an employer or friend when you were an adult. Have each person *who chooses to do so,* share their experience. Review the suggestions for correcting misbehavior in Task 5 and discuss whether or not the guidelines presented there might have made the unskillful feedback more positive learning experiences.

2. Have each person share any useful ideas that were gained from working through the **Take Action** activity for this chapter. Have those who wish to do so share their goals for increasing positive interactions with certain students and identify how they will monitor their progress toward their goals. NOTE: Individuals may wish to "pair up" and arrange to check-in with each other in 3 or 4 weeks to see how they are doing.

CHAPTER 4

Supervising Common Areas

Common areas are locations in the school where students from many different classrooms may be present—for example, the cafeteria, the hallways and restrooms, the playground, and the bus loading/unloading area(s). As a paraeducator, there is a high probability that at one time or another you will be assigned to supervise a common area. Supervising a common area such as the playground is sometimes referred to as "having playground duty."

Common area supervision can be one of the most challenging assignments for any school staff member. On the playground, for instance, there may be 150 or more students—and only two adults. These adults are responsible for correcting misbehavior, dealing with scraped knees and hurt feelings, talking to students who need attention, and making sure that students are playing safely. Yet, as challenging as this assignment can be, supervising a common area can also be very rewarding. You get to know many different children. You help set a positive climate for the school. You help ensure that students are safe from emotional and physical harm. And you get to spend time with students when they are more relaxed and socializing—on the playground, in the cafeteria, or at the end of the day as they are waiting for buses to arrive.

This chapter has three tasks. The first involves getting key information about the common area setting you will be supervising—what the expectations for you are, what the expectations for students are, and what procedures you are to use for handling emergencies. The second task deals with knowing how to supervise any common area—that is, it has information on monitoring student behavior (circulating and scanning), reinforcing responsible behavior, and responding effectively to misbehavior in common areas. The last task has to do with being aware of specific management tips that apply to cafeterias, to playgrounds, and to hallways and restrooms, respectively. We suggest that you carefully read through Tasks 1 and 2, and then skim the section(s) in Task 3 related to the particular common area(s) for which you have supervisory responsibility.

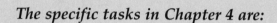

The specific tasks in Chapter 4 are:

1. **Know the procedures and expectations for each common area you supervise.**

2. **Know how to effectively supervise any common area for which you have responsibility.**

3. **Be aware of specific management tips that apply to: the cafeteria, the playground, and the hallways and restrooms.**

PROFESSIONAL

PLANFUL · POSITIVE

PATIENT · PERSISTENT

TASK 1:

Know the procedures and expectations for each common area you supervise.

To effectively supervise a common area, you need to know as much about the setting as possible. That is why we have highlighted the Planful point of the five-point star. And, in order to find out what is expected of you for any particular assignment, you need to know who your supervisor is for that assignment—which can be especially unclear when it comes to common areas. Furthermore, it is quite possible that your supervisor for a common area will not be the person to train you and "show you the ropes." Your orientation to the tasks and responsibilities of common area supervision, in fact, may fall to an experienced paraeducator. Keep in mind that if your supervisor has given authority for training you to someone else, you need to treat that person with respect and be prepared to learn as much as you can from him or her.

During your training and orientation to common area supervision, pay careful attention and ask lots of questions. On the following pages you will find a reproducible form, Figure 4.1, designed to help you identify the kind of key information you will need for any common area. Make a copy of this form for each common area you will supervise, and complete it during your training and orientation for that setting.

If you are put in a situation where you don't get any training or information before you actually have to supervise an area, do your best. Use the first few days to observe the other duty supervisors and to ask them questions about the issues on the form. As the days progress, you should be able to get all the information necessary to complete the form.

If there's a procedure or way of doing things that you don't particularly like, do not change it without prior approval of your supervisor. As you learn the basics of supervising a particular common area, you may come up with some good ideas for improving the setting. Before offering your suggestions, however, carefully consider all of the ramifications. Think about how to propose the changes in a helpful, rather than critical, manner and be prepared to accept it if your suggestions are not accepted. Finally, avoid the temptation to compare this school assignment with others you may have had in the past, because each school is different.

There is no "How To Do It" section for this task. Instead, we simply recommend that you complete the following worksheet (or something similar) for each common area you will be supervising. If you already have experience supervising a particular common area, use the worksheet to identify any gaps in your knowledge of the key information about that setting.

Common Area Supervision: Procedures and Expectations

Area: _____

Supervisor: _____ Time: _____

BASIC PROCEDURES:

- While I am on duty, where should I leave personal possessions (e.g., purse, teaching materials)?

- What tools are needed for supervising this area (e.g., walkie-talkie, whistle, clipboard)? Where do I get these tools? Where do I store these tools at the end of the supervision period?

- Are there any forms, recording sheets, or other paperwork I should have with me? If so, how do I use these materials?

- If I notice vandalism or other damage in the setting, to whom and when do I report it?

- Other considerations:

EMERGENCY PROCEDURES:

- How do I let the office know that an emergency situation exists?

- What is the backup plan if the first communication procedures do not work?

- What do I do if there is a fire drill?

- What are the "lockdown" procedures and/or "safe zones" for students (e.g., if there is a report that someone has a weapon)?

- What are the natural disaster procedures (e.g., tornado plans)?

- Who do I contact about a health emergency? What are the procedures?

- Who do I contact for other possible emergency situations (e.g., a suspicious acting stranger is just outside the boundary of the playground)? What are the procedures?

- What do I do if two students are physically fighting?

BEHAVIORAL AND SUPERVISORY EXPECTATIONS:

- Where and how do students enter the setting? Do I have any special responsibilities for assisting with students' entry?

- How do students demonstrate appropriate behavior in this setting?
  (NOTE: This may be especially complex on playgrounds.)

- Are there areas/situations to which I should plan on paying particular attention (e.g., known trouble spots)?

- What predictable misbehaviors should I be prepared to correct?

- What correction procedures/corrective consequences are recommended for this setting? not recommended and/or specifically to be avoided?

- How do students exit this setting? What are my responsibilities for dismissing students or helping with the transition? (e.g., do I have to watch dismissal time, or is there a bell or some other cue?)

- Have the behavioral expectations for this setting been taught to students? What responsibility do I have in terms of communicating (e.g., teaching, reviewing) the expectations to students?

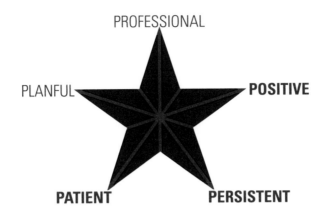

PROFESSIONAL

PLANFUL

POSITIVE

PATIENT

PERSISTENT

TASK 2:

Know how to effectively supervise any common area for which you have responsibility.

When you supervise in a common area, you serve many roles. You are there to ensure school safety, to reinforce school rules, and to build relationships with the students. All these roles are important and all play a part in keeping common areas safe and orderly.

For this task, we have highlighted three points of the star. Effective supervision in common areas requires that you be positive. Your behavior (and that of the other supervisors in the setting) sets a tone. It can be a tone of high expectations, cooperation, and respect—or it can be a tone of hostility, negative expectations, and antagonism. Keep your focus on the positive—smile and be friendly. Persistence is also critical because, no matter how well you supervised yesterday, every day is a new day when it comes to student behavior. You need to stay active, cover the area, watch for situations that need intervention and remain vigilant at all times. Finally, you need to be patient. Students will make errors and will occasionally break the

rules, and you will be a more effective supervisor if you are patient when you correct them.

In the "How To Do It" section of this task, we offer general suggestions that will help you with the supervision of any common area.

(NOTE: In Task 3, you will find management tips for specific common areas.)

HOW TO DO IT:

• Be on time.

When you have supervisory responsibility for a common area, you should be in that setting before the students arrive. Because your main responsibility is student safety, you need to actually be at the setting in the unlikely event that an emergency should occur in the first two minutes of the recess or lunch period, for example. In addition, when you appear on the scene after the students, your first interaction with them is more likely to be corrective than inviting. There may be times when scheduling puts you in an unreasonable position—that is, you are scheduled to be in a classroom until 10:15 and to be on the playground starting at 10:15. It's not possible for you to get from the classroom to the playground in zero seconds. If you have a schedule with no "travel time" built in, talk to your primary supervisor and ask for help in resolving the situation.

• Establish a positive expectation from the moment students arrive.

When your first contact with students is positive, you reduce the potential for misbehavior. Smile and provide a friendly greeting to as many students as possible as they arrive at the setting. Use the students' names to greet them. (Initially you probably won't know all the students' names, but try to learn the names of a few more students each day.) One very experienced paraeducator knows all the students in her 450-student elementary school so well that if a student is absent for a few days, she notices. When that student returns to school, she goes to the student on the playground or the cafeteria (she has both duties) and says, "Yvette, you weren't here for a couple of days. I missed you and it is good to have you back." Remember, all that's required is a warm, friendly greeting in a manner that fits your personal style.

Make a special effort to seek out and greet students who have had previous problems in that setting. Spend a moment and talk to the student about one or more of the student's interests. This shows the student that you don't hold a grudge for past behavior or have a negative expectation of him, and it gives the student some attention while he is behaving responsibly. It also helps you build a positive relationship with the student. While there is no guarantee that the student will behave responsibly for the rest of the time in that setting, this kind of contact and attention increases the chances that he will.

• Actively monitor the setting.

During the entire time you are on duty in a common area, keep your attention focused on students. Your goal is to be "in touch" with what is going on in all the different locations and with all the different students you have responsibility for at that time. This means that no single event or person should ever have your full and undivided attention.

Constant visual scanning is the most important tool in your repertoire as you supervise. If you are talking with an individual student, you can occasionally say, "Excuse me a second," and then visually sweep across the setting to see what else is going on. On the playground, if you stop to watch a soccer game for a minute or two, turn around every 30 seconds or so and check out what is happening in other parts of the playground. If several supervisors have divided up locations within a setting (e.g., three supervisors each take one-third of the cafeteria), occasionally scan into the other supervisors' sections just to make sure that they are not in need of any assistance.

Circulating (moving purposefully throughout the area you are supervising) is also an important strategy. Your physical proximity serves as a reminder to students to follow the rules. As much as possible, anticipate potential problems and spend slightly more time in areas that you know tend to be more problematic. For example, you may know that in the cafeteria certain students routinely bother other students seated at

Keep moving and keep your eyes and ears open.

the table near the exit. Make a point to be near that table when this is most likely to happen. Or, when supervising the playground, if you know that there tends to be more conflicts in the kickball game than on the blacktop area, spend more time being physically close to the kickball game, while you visually scan the blacktop.

Another aspect of anticipating potential trouble spots is to "read" what is happening as you circulate, scan, and listen. This is hard to describe exactly, but the more experienced you become, the more skilled you will be at picking up slightly increased movement or different noise levels or giggling or other signs that tell you trouble is percolating in a particular section of the setting you are supervising. When you pick up on these subtle cues, go to that area. Spend some time there, talk with students—potential trouble will likely be averted because your presence serves as a gentle reminder to follow the rules.

Avoid being predictable as you circulate. For example, if you are a campus monitor (security) in a high school, students should not be able to predict where you will be. When students know where you generally are between third and fourth period, then they also know where you generally are not—and that is where the students with the greatest tendency to push limits are likely to be.

When you are monitoring students in a line (e.g., in a cafeteria or bus loading area), "work the line"—that is, circulate up and down the line and between multiple lines—interacting with students, asking them about their day and using the time to build relationships with them.

Do not let other adults in the setting stop you from circulating and scanning. If a staff friend, who is not on duty at the time, comes to visit with you while you are on duty, say hello, then skillfully and diplomatically say good-bye. In some cases, another duty supervisor may want to spend the time talking to you. Be kind but assertive, and let that person know that you need to keep circulating. Keep on the move and keep your focus of attention on the students.

In addition to monitoring student behavior, you also want to watch out for potential major emergencies. These might include a suspicious-acting stranger just outside the playground area, an overheard statement that a student may have a weapon or drugs, or a student with a health emergency. If you are prepared with information on emergency procedures and communication networks (see Task 1), then follow through on those procedures. If something is happening and you are not sure how to handle it, contact another duty supervisor or the principal or assistant principal.

• Model the behaviors you want to see.

Don't just tell students what to do, demonstrate it for them. If you ask a student to pick up some litter on the playground, pick up some yourself so the student sees that this expectation holds true for everyone. If you want students to use a quiet voice in the cafeteria, use a quiet voice yourself when you greet students, when you give positive feedback, when you correct misbehavior, and even when you speak with other adults. If students hear you using a booming voice all the time, they will be more likely to use a booming voice. If you expect students to treat you with respect, they should see you treating them with respect.

• Interact positively and reinforce responsible behavior.

As students enter the setting, set a positive tone with greetings and positive feedback. "Jamal, how are you today? Gina, Elkie, Beth, thanks for walking as you come into the cafeteria. Therese, it's good to see you." Providing greetings and positive feedback as students enter accomplishes several important things. It gives students attention in a way that demonstrates they do not have to misbehave to be noticed. It contributes to a positive climate in the setting. It helps you build relationships with the students you supervise. And last, but definitely not least, it lets students know that adults are present to enforce rules and provide help if needed.

109

Be careful not to embarrass students with praise. Singling out one individual for praise may be embarrassing, so praise groups of students. "Everyone here at the four square game is demonstrating cooperation and respect. Great job, folks." "It's good to see all of you. Thanks for keeping the noise level down at this table." Use nonverbal interactions as well. Smiles, nods, winks, and thumbs up signs effectively communicate to a student or a group, "I notice that you are following the rules in this setting."

When you want to give positive feedback to an individual, do it somewhat privately. For example, say a student who has had trouble in the bus loading area is behaving responsibly. As he is moving toward the bus, quietly tell the student, "You are being respectful of others by keeping your hands to yourself. Thanks."

In Chapter 3, we introduced the idea of making a conscious effort to interact at least three times more frequently with every student when he or she is engaged in positive behavior than when he or she is engaged in negative behavior. Greetings, smiles, winks, nods, and verbal praise are considered "positives," because each involves giving attention to a student while the student is behaving responsibly. "Negatives" are behaviors like giving reminders, implementing correction procedures, and "giving the eye" (looking at a student engaged in misbehavior in a way that gets the student to cease the misbehavior) because they all involve attention to irresponsible behavior. "Negatives" are a necessary part of supervising common areas, but if your "negatives" outnumber your "positives," then you need to decrease the number of negatives and increase the number of positives. This is important not only because your behavior contributes to the climate (positive or negative) in your school, but also because students need to see that it is easier to get your attention for positive behavior than for negative behavior.

—Respond effectively to student misbehavior.

Misbehavior is going to occur in common areas. No matter how much students have been taught the rules, or have been reinforced for behaving

responsibly, or have had their irresponsible behavior corrected in the past, misbehavior will still happen. That is one of the reasons you are supervising—to enforce the rules and to do something about the rule breaking that does occur. Some people may ask, "Why can't we just get kids to behave without needing supervision and rules and corrections?" The answer is that human nature is such that people tend to push limits and occasionally break a rule. Think about interstate highways. Why are there police officers, speed limits, and speeding tickets? The answer is, because many people (even really fine, ethical, honest people) drive too fast sometimes. However, speed limits, highway patrol officers, and speeding tickets help keep the rule breaking to a manageable level. Don't get frustrated—just keep reminding yourself that enforcing the rules is part of why you are there. Following are some general tips for responding to misbehavior in a variety of common area settings.

—Use proximity management.

Physically move toward where the misbehavior is occurring. Monitor your body language carefully. Do not convey that you are upset by how you walk or how you hold your arms. If the misbehavior ceases by the time you get there, say something like, "Now you are acting responsibly."

—Give positive feedback to students near the area of misbehavior.

Giving positive feedback to students exhibiting responsible behavior may prompt a student engaged in misbehavior to begin meeting the positive expectations. For example, if one student is using too loud of a voice and you praise other nearby students for using their "indoor voices," you may find that the first student lowers her voice as well. This is most effective with primary age students.

—When you speak to a student about misbehavior, do it as privately as possible.

When correcting a student, the physical positioning of where you stand and where the student stands is very important. Move the student away from friends and position him so that he is facing slightly away from the crowd and so that you are facing somewhat toward the crowd. (NOTE: This may be easier to accomplish by having the crowd move.) Stand slightly off to the side of the student rather than "squared off" in a sort of fighting stance. This reduces the possibility that your interaction with the student will turn into a battle of wills and allows you to continue to scan the setting. Positioning the student facing somewhat away from the crowd reduces the student's need to "play to the audience." That is, when a student is positioned so that he can see other students and other students can see him, he is less likely to think about what you are saying because he is too busy thinking about how he looks in front of his friends.

WHEN CORRECTING AN INDIVIDUAL STUDENT, POSITION THE STUDENT SO HE IS FACING AWAY FROM OTHER STUDENTS AND YOURSELF SO THAT YOU ARE FACING THE STUDENT AND CAN SEE THE SETTING. AVOID A CONFRONTATIONAL, "SQUARED-OFF," STANCE TOWARD THE STUDENT.

—*Don't ask students to tattle on other students.*

If you hear a swear word on the playground but are not sure who said it, do not go to the gener-

al area and ask, "Who said that?" First of all, you probably won't get the information, which will put you in an awkward position. Or, you may get one student accusing another, which can actually cause more problems. If you try to correct the accused student and he or she denies the behavior, you may find yourself in a cycle of accusations and denials that will be impossible to sort out. In addition, the situation may create tension between students that could lead to later intimidation or fighting. In a case like this, simply go over to the group and make a statement like, "That language is inappropriate." Then walk away. Do not get into an argument or power struggle. If the students respond that they didn't say anything, you can say something like, "Good, because you need to be using school language." Make a point to monitor that area more closely in the future.

In addition to the preceding general tips for dealing with misbehavior in common areas, following are suggestions for specific correction strategies that may be useful in those settings.

—*Use a gentle reprimand.*

Simply remind students of what they should be doing. A variation of this would be to say to the student, "Tell me what the expectation is." If the student responds inappropriately, state the expectation yourself. Don't debate or try to "pull the information" out of the student.

—*Briefly delay the student.*

On a playground, for example, you might tell a student to stand in place and think about the rule that was broken. After 15 seconds or so, have the student tell you what she should do differently, then send her on her way. This is a very easy-to-implement correction that can be used in all common areas. It is surprisingly effective because it is mildly inconveniencing to the student.

—*Change the location.*

Have the student move to a different location and make the location of the misbehavior off limits for the rest of that time period. For example, if a student on the playground is having trouble behaving in the soccer game, tell the student she needs to stay on the blacktop area and make soccer off limits for the student for the rest of that recess time. In a cafeteria, you might have a student take his lunch and move to a different table.

—Assign a brief time-out.

Have the student go to a particular area and do nothing for three minutes. For example, if a student is misbehaving in the cafeteria and a reprimand has not been effective, you could have the student leave the table and stand in a low-traffic area of the cafeteria for a brief period. Before

allowing the student to return to his table, have him tell you the expected behavior. Remember, there shouldn't be more than one student in the time-out area at any one time.

—Have the student spend time with you (the supervisor).

Let the student know that since he is having trouble behaving responsibly without supervision, he needs to stay with you so that you can supervise him. This is especially effective for students who get a lot of attention for their misbehavior from peers.

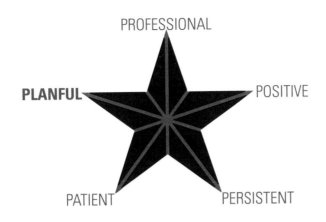

PROFESSIONAL

PLANFUL

POSITIVE

PATIENT

PERSISTENT

TASK 3:

Be aware of specific management tips that apply to: the cafeteria, the playground, and the hallways and restrooms.

*R*eview any written policies and procedures your school may have for the specific common area(s) you will be supervising. These may appear in a staff handbook or as part of the school's behavior management and discipline policies. Unfortunately, often these materials do not address exactly what you need to do or how you need to do it. Therefore, you may find the following specific management tips for cafeterias, playgrounds, and hallways and restrooms to be useful. You need to read only those sections that apply to the common area(s) you will be supervising. Also, be sure to discuss the suggestions with your supervisor and others who have the same common area duty before implementing them.

NOTE: In some of the sections you will find references to video inservice material that your supervisor or an administrator may wish to preview. All the recommended materials have been designed to help schools improve the safety of their common areas.

HOW TO DO IT:

• **Be aware of some specific management tips that apply to cafeterias.**

One area of potential trouble in cafeterias is the line of students waiting to get their lunches. Arrange with other cafeteria supervisors to have one person "work the line." This means that you (or one of the other duty supervisors) meets and greets students as they enter the cafeteria. Then, you keep moving up and down the line interacting with students. Your presence will reduce the probability that any students will try to "cut in line," and it should reduce horseplay such as pushing or poking. If a couple of the students in line are having trouble (arguing, pushing, or being too loud), separate them by having one of the students move farther back in the line. Creating distance between the students often eliminates the problem. When monitoring a line of students in fourth grade and below, you might want to inform them of any lunch choices that day. This can help the line move faster because the students will be able to think about their choice before getting to the serving area.

If your school does not currently have an "attention signal" for getting students quiet when the noise becomes excessive or you need to make an announcement, you might want to propose the idea to your supervisor. One signal idea is to raise one hand and hold up two fingers to indicate that it needs to get a little bit quieter or hold up one finger to indicate that it needs to be completely quiet. Another signal involves flicking the overhead lights to indicate that it needs to get quieter or turning one bank of lights off to indicate the need for complete silence. If you implement the signal for silence, use a stopwatch to time how long it takes for all conversation to cease, then give the students feedback. If it takes longer than 10 to 15 seconds, tell students they need to work on getting silent quicker. If it takes less than 10 to 15 seconds, compliment the students. Once students are silent, make whatever announcements you need to make. If you use the signal to reduce the noise level and students do not respond to the "get quieter" signal, have them stay completely silent for about a minute as a minor correction.

Encourage polite behavior in the cafeteria—that is, the use of "Please," "Thank you," and "Excuse me." When you notice a student being polite, provide age-appropriate positive feedback. When a student fails to use the basic courtesies, prompt him or her by saying, "Say 'please' when you ask someone to pass something to you at the table."

If students are expected to clean up their own messes in the cafeteria, make sure they do so. Sometimes it may feel as though it would be easier to clean up a student's mess, but doing that is a disservice to that student. If you clean up for a student, she may begin to think that she does not have to be responsible for herself. So, even though it may be more work, be persistent in having students take care of their own messes.

If students need permission from a duty supervisor to be excused, make sure that you only respond to students when they signal you in the correct way. For example, say students are expected to raise their hand and wait for you to come over and check their area for neatness. Make sure you watch for and promptly excuse students with their hands up, and that you ignore or reprimand students who call out to you. This shows that the only way you will excuse students is if they follow the established procedures. If all the students at one table have repeatedly been too noisy, you might delay excusing the entire table. Tell the students that the expectation is for them to sit quietly, then quickly start excusing those students who are meeting this expectation.

Some "one-liners" that are effective for preventing and/or dealing with misbehavior in the cafeteria are:

—*Keep your hands to yourself.*

—*Pick up your tray and walk with me.*

—*Voice levels are too loud. Bring them down, please.*

—*Stand (or sit) here. I'll talk to you as soon as I can.*

Other tips that are useful when supervising the cafeteria include making sure you have the information about where students are to go when they have finished eating. Students are likely to ask, especially on days with inclement weather. Also, if you have not had training in how to deal with a person who is choking on food, ask your supervisor if you can get this training. District or community health professionals are a good resource for this type of training. Finally (please bear with this particular pet peeve of the authors), when monitoring a waste disposal area, don't tell students to "dump" their trays—that sounds tacky. Consider saying something like, "clean your tray" or "dispose of the waste."

NOTE: If it seems appropriate, you may want to suggest that your supervisor or administrator preview the following video inservice program:

Cafeteria Discipline: Positive Techniques for Lunchroom Supervision

R. S. Sprick. (1995). Eugene, OR: Teaching Strategies.

• Be aware of some specific management tips that apply to playgrounds.

Playgrounds give students an opportunity to relax and to practice social skills. However, playgrounds can be complex and they have more potential for safety problems than most other common areas. The following suggestions can help you make your playground(s) safe and problem-free.

Know the boundaries of the playground setting so you can consistently intervene if a student goes into an off-limits area. Often they will be defined, at least in part, by a fence. However, there may be boundaries that are not as well defined. For example, many schools have "portable classrooms," and you need to know whether students are allowed to go near those portables during their time on the playground.

Know the rules for games and equipment. If these are not written anywhere, you will have to learn them from the students and other staff. (NOTE: We do recommend that the rules be written down at some point to increase staff's ability to provide consistent instruction and supervision to students. See the Playground Discipline program referenced at the end of this section.)

Watch out for strangers or vehicles on the perimeter of the playground. Immediately report any suspicious activity to the office. If you are comfortable with it, occasionally join students in a game for a few minutes. This demonstrates that you enjoy being out there and enjoy being with the students. Do this only when things are very calm on other parts of the playground and don't get so into the game that you forget to scan. After two minutes or so, thank the students for letting you join in, excuse yourself, and move to a different part of the playground.

If you use the "Stay with me" correction strategy for a misbehavior (see page 112), have the student who is walking with you point out rules and expectations (e.g., have the student describe the rules for appropriate play in tether ball, four square, soccer, etc.).

If a student has had several behavior problems while participating in a particular game, make that game "off limits" for the student. Football, basketball, and dodgeball all tend to be very competitive and all tend to involve lots of physical contact, which some students have difficulty handling. If there's a student who continually exhibits behaviors such as fighting, arguing, or bullying during one of these games, make the game off limits until the student can demonstrate responsible play in less volatile games. Encourage the student to play tetherball, foursquare, and other games with less contact. Praise the student for staying calm and playing fairly. When the student has demonstrated responsible behavior for at least three days, ask the student if he thinks he can rejoin the original (problematic) game without problems. Give the student some suggestions for being successful. "Be less concerned about winning and losing." "Be calm and have fun." Let the student know that if there are any further problems, the game will become off limits for an even longer period next time.

Tattling tends to be a big problem on many playgrounds. Responding thoughtfully is critical. If a student tells you about another student who is injured or some other immediate and visible problem, thank the student for helping. If a student tells you about another student who broke the rules, say something like, "I am glad you know the rules," and then tell the student you will monitor the situation.

If a student tells you that another student is bullying or threatening her, help the student figure out strategies for dealing with the problem. For example, you might suggest that the student stay away from the bully or that the student stay closer to where you are supervising so that you will be able to see if any bullying takes place. Let the student know that you will be watching her to see if she needs help. If several students report that a particular student has been bothering them, keep a very close eye on that student. If the reports continue and/or you are witness to a bullying incident, talk to your supervisor about whether the building principal or school counselor should be made aware of the problem.

Some "one-liners" that are effective for preventing and/or dealing with misbehavior on the playground are:

—*Tell me (or show me) the right way to . . . .*

—*This game is off limits for the remainder of recess.*

—*Take a time out and when I get back, be ready to tell me what you need to do.*

—*At this time, either play responsibly or move to another game.*

—*It looks like you're having fun, but you need to find something else to do.*

There are special considerations for the end of recess periods. For example, if your school recess procedures do not currently include a transition area, you may wish to suggest the concept to your supervisor. A transition area is a place where students line up before they are dismissed into the building. Generally students wait in lines, by classroom, until their teachers come out to meet them and escort them, still in lines, back to their classrooms. Transition areas help create a calm transition from the activity of recess to the more controlled behavior required in a classroom. Without a transition area, entry from recess can be rambunctious and boisterous, with students racing and pushing their way into the building.

At the end of recess, walk with any stragglers and model for them how to hurry back toward the building or transition area without running. If one (or more) student has a repeated problem with straggling, have the student(s) stay with you at the beginning of the next recess. Tell the student that whenever he wastes time at the end of one recess, you will have him stay with you for the same amount of time at the beginning of the next recess. If several students are having a problem with straggling, use a stopwatch for a couple of days and record how long it is taking after the signal occurs for all students to be in lines (or back in the building). Share the information with your supervisor, and discuss how

to handle the problem. It may be that the principal needs to talk to students over the intercom about the problem or perhaps the principal needs to talk to teachers about teaching their students the end-of-recess procedures.

If you have a transition area, work the lines, interacting with students and giving students positive feedback. When the teachers arrive, formally hand over authority by saying something like, "Please listen to your teacher for directions." Find out from your supervisor what to do if a teacher is late in picking up the students. This is especially important if you have to report to a different location after recess or if another group of students will be coming out to recess. When a teacher (or teachers) is repeatedly late to pick up his class, report the problem to your supervisor and ask how the situation can be resolved.

Additional information on structuring and organizing a playground and on training playground supervisors can be found in the video program:

Playground Discipline: Positive Techniques for Playground Supervision

R.S. Sprick. (1990). Eugene, OR: Teaching Strategies.

If your school seems to have an ongoing problem with students who tease and bully, you may wish to suggest that someone in authority review:

Bully-Proofing Your School

C. Carrity, K. Jens, W. Porter, N. Sager, and C. Short-Camilli. (1994)

Longmont, CO: Sopris West.

• **Be aware of some specific management tips that apply to** *hallways and restrooms.*

When you have responsibility for supervising hallways, it's important to be in the hall before or as students enter if at all possible. If you don't arrive until after students are present, trouble could already be brewing.

When supervising a hallway, stand in the middle of the hall. This makes you more visible and it defines the center, which will make a "Walk on the right" expectation more clearly defined. If you have to get to a class after the passing period, occasionally move from the middle of the hall to the doorway of the classroom to check on any students in the classroom. Continue to monitor both the classroom and the hall.

As you supervise the halls, interact with the students—greetings, nods, and eye contact all help establish a positive tone and communicate that you are aware of students when they are behaving positively. Whenever possible, intervene early at any sign of horseplay—pushing, loud voices, disrespect, and so on. If you can intervene while the behavior is at a low level, a gentle reminder may be all that is necessary to get students to settle down or to disperse. However, once things intensify, even for a couple of minutes, a momentum of misbehavior can build that may result in the students being defiant or ignoring you altogether.

Practiced "one-liners" that are effective for hallways include: "It's time to go to class." "Keep moving, please." "Hands, feet, and objects to yourself." As the passing period is ending, give students prompts. Note that something like, "Class begins in about 30 seconds" is a better cue than " Don't be late for class." Give any prompts in a firm but friendly manner.

If your supervisory duties include monitoring the halls during "non-passing periods" (e.g., when class is in session) and your school requires students to have a hall pass to be in the halls or restrooms during class times, be sure to check the hall pass of any student in the halls. If the student does not have a hall pass, direct him or her back to class or escort the student to the office.

If you see an adult you don't know in the halls, check to see if the person has a visitor badge. If not, let the person know that visitors are required to check in at the office before being allowed in the school. If possible, escort the person to the office. If that is not possible, head the person in the direction of the office and as soon as possible let the office know that someone should make sure the stranger has checked in.

Be sure to ask your supervisor about the policies and procedures for restroom supervision. For example, you need to know details such as: whether going into same-gender restrooms is part of your supervision responsibilities; if you should stand outside opposite-gender restrooms to listen for any inappropriate activity (e.g., horseplay, splashing water); what you should do if you suspect that something inappropriate is going on (e.g., you smell cigarette smoke); whether you should check restrooms for vandalism, messes, or other damage after classes have begun; and how you should follow up on student reports of damage or problems that might be taking place.

CHAPTER 4 ★ ACTIVITIES

THINK ABOUT IT

Use the following chart to evaluate your familiarity with the material presented in this chapter. When you have completed this activity, enter reminders about the tasks you wanted to reread or discuss into your planning calendar.

Figure 4.2 Reproducible Form

	The information was not applicable to my situation.	The information was familiar. I consistently implement the strategies presented.	The information was useful. I should reread this task at least once more this year.	Some of the information was new. I should reread this task within a month.	Much of the information was new. I should discuss it with my supervisor or with other paraeducators.
TASK 1: Know the procedures and expectations for each common area you supervise.	0	1	2	3	4
TASK 2: Know how to effectively supervise any common area for which you have responsibility.	0	1	2	3	4
TASK 3: Be aware of specific management tips that apply to: the cafeteria, the playground, and the hallways and restrooms.	0	1	2	3	4

(NOTE: On pages 205-210, in the back of the book, you will find a complete chart of all the tasks in the book. You may wish to summarize the information from each individual chapter on this single chart.)

TAKE ACTION

Use the Common Area Supervision Checklist (Figure 4.3) to help you identify those supervision techniques you implement well and those on which you need to improve. Make 2 copies of the reproducible Checklist. Use one copy to rate yourself—putting a "+" next to each technique you implement consistently and a "0" next to each technique that you either do not implement or implement inconsistently. Also ask a supervisor or a peer to observe you as you supervise and rate you on the other copy of the Checklist. Meet with the other person and compare the two evaluations. Discuss your strengths, areas that need improvement, and any discrepancies. Use the information to set some improvement goals for yourself. You may wish to check back with the individual in 3 or 4 weeks to give a progress report. (NOTE: Paraeducators who have daily common area supervision responsibilities should consider having two observations a year—the first around the sixth week of school and the second in the middle of the year.)

Common Area Supervision Checklist

Setting: _____

_____ I always intentionally meet students in a welcoming and positive manner as they enter the setting I supervise—that is, I am positive, I smile, and I call students by name.

_____ I am always on time for my supervision responsibility.

_____ I always intentionally meet students in a welcoming and positive manner as they enter the setting—that is, I am positive, I smile, and I call students by name.

_____ I intentionally seek out students who have difficulty in the setting within the first 5 minutes. I positively connect with each of these students by smiling, making a positive comment, and/or briefly talking about something that interests the student.

_____ When correcting a student's misbehavior, I always position the student so that I can continue to effectively supervise—that is, so that the student's back is to the group and I am facing the group.

_____ I only leave the area I am supervising to deal with an emergency after I have told another adult. If I am the only adult on duty, I consider directing a responsible student to get help instead of leaving myself.

_____ I immediately ask my supervisor if I have any questions/concerns or if I need clarification regarding my supervision assignment.

_____ I am always on the move in the area I supervise. I move intentionally as well as continuously and I monitor my movement so that students cannot detect a pattern.

_____ I move through all sections of my assigned area, regardless of the surface in that area (i.e., mud, bark mulch, gravel, etc.).

_____ I move close to students who are beginning to have difficulties and I stay longer in "problem" areas so that students are aware that I am monitoring.

_____ I never allow other adults to usurp my time either when I am on my way to my assignment or while I am supervising.

_____ I am purposeful about looking around at all students in the area and intentionally make sure that I do not just look at one area or in one direction.

_____ I am always on the move in the area I supervise. I move intentionally as well as continuously and I monitor my movement so that students cannot detect a pattern.

_____ I step in at the onset of any potential problem.

_____ I make a point of being more positive than corrective when interacting with students overall, and particularly with students who have difficulty in the area.

_____ I give students specific, descriptive praise that is age appropriate and they can tell that I am sincere.

_____ I never (or rarely) use an unprofessional tone with students and I always use a supportive stance (i.e., off to one side, not directly in front) when I talk to individual students.

_____ I always use an instructional approach when I correct misbehavior. That is, I state the rule for the student, or have the student tell me the rule, or have the student demonstrate the correct behavior.

Strengths *(effective practices I want to applaud myself for):*

Goals *(supervision techniques I want to improve):*

DISCUSS IT

Arrange with a group of colleagues to read Chapter 4 and do the Take Action activity for this chapter. Then schedule a meeting at which the group can discuss the following topics/questions.

1. Review the reproducible worksheet in Figure 4.3 (pages 120-121). If you are not able to answer all of the questions/issues on the worksheet, decide whether or not, as a group, you should ask a supervisor or the building principal for assistance.

2. Have each person in the group share any ideas about how to improve one or more of the school's common areas—based on the information presented in the chapter. Decide whether or not, as a group, you should share these ideas with a supervisor or the building principal for staff consideration.

3. Have each person share any useful ideas that were gained from working through the Take Action activity for this chapter. What goals did each person set for himself/herself? Discuss what affect these goals may have on student behavior in the common area(s).

CHAPTER 5

Working with Small Groups

In many schools, paraeducators are assigned to work with one or more small groups of students. Sometimes these are regularly scheduled assignments. For example, every day you work with one small group in the classroom while the teacher works with another. In other cases, you may be asked to work with a small group for a specific occasion. For example, the teacher asks you to work with four to six students who need extra help to review for a test the next day. The tasks in this chapter are geared to someone who works with a small group on a regular basis, but the information and suggestions can help anyone who works with a small group in any situation.

It is important to note that even when you work directly with a small group, the responsibility for student learning belongs to your immediate supervisor for that time period (i.e., your supervising teacher). That is, it is your job to support instruction and your supervising teacher's job to make decisions about placement and grouping, materials to be used with the group, what to do if one or more students have difficulty with the material, and so on. As you consider the information in this chapter, remember that you need to confer with your supervising teacher prior to implementing any of the suggestions and that you need to leave all final decisions to your supervisor.

The specific tasks in Chapter 5 are:

1. Know the procedures, materials, and what is expected of you.

2. Know the behavioral expectations for students.

3. Teach the behavioral expectations to students (as needed).

4. Use effective instructional techniques.

5. Manage student behavior effectively.

NOTE: Throughout the chapter, we refer to working with a group. If you work with more than one group, the suggestions would apply to each group with which you work.

PROFESSIONAL

PLANFUL

POSITIVE

PATIENT

PERSISTENT

TASK 1:

Know the procedures, materials, and what is expected of you.

Working effectively with a small group requires that you be planful—that is, that you get a lot of information from your immediate supervisor for that time period. In addition to procedures and expectations, the information you need includes knowing about the materials that will be used during any lessons. Once you know this information in full detail, you will be able to work with your group in a way that maximizes your supervising teacher's effectiveness in achieving the educational objectives for the students in that group.

Remember, your supervisor is responsible for making decisions about placement, grouping, instructional materials, instructional strategies, and so on. Your responsibility is to carry out those decisions. If you are not sure about any aspect of your work with a small group, ask your supervisor. If you come up with ideas that

you think might improve the group, be sure to discuss them with your supervisor before taking action. Thoughtfully present any suggestions in a constructive, rather than critical, manner, and be prepared to accept it should your supervisor choose not to implement the suggestions.

The "How To Do It" section of this task walks you through the kinds of information you should get from your supervising teacher. The task ends with a reproducible worksheet, Figure 5. 2 on page 131, that you can use as an interview form to guide your discussion with your supervisor.

(NOTE: Task 2 in this chapter covers the information you will need regarding the behavioral expectations your supervisor has for the students. It, too, ends with a reproducible worksheet that you can use in your conversation with your supervisor.)

HOW TO DO IT:

• **Find out the time schedule for the small group and your responsibilities for getting students to and from the group.**

Once you know when your small group is supposed to begin and end, look at your schedule and make sure there is time for you to transition from one assignment to another. For example, if your schedule has you working with a small group in the resource room from 9:45 to 10:30 and doing playground duty from 10:30 to 10:45, you will need to ask for help from your primary supervisor.

If you work in a resource or Title 1 room and have a group of students who come from different classrooms, you will also need to find out whether you are expected to pick the students up from and escort them back to their classes. If so, make sure your schedule includes this time. If the students are responsible for getting to the group on their own, ask your supervisor how to handle students who arrive late. Often, with this type of problem, your supervisor will need to talk to the students' classroom teachers about sending the students from the classroom before the group's scheduled start time. (You can help by remembering to give students positive feedback for being on time to your group.)

Whenever you work with a small group, be sure to start and stop the group at the designated times. Don't forget that what you do with your group has an impact on others. That is, if your group runs five minutes too long, that throws off the schedules of the teachers who work with the students next.

- **Find out what instructional materials you will be using and what kind of training on using the materials is available to you.**

Most paraeducators who work with a small group on a regular basis are given a program or set of materials (i.e., a curriculum) to use. Being familiar with the materials you will be working with will improve your effectiveness when doing small group work. Ask your supervising teacher if you can look over the materials prior to starting with your group. Also ask about available training options on how to use the material most effectively. Typically this can include: a) detailed written manuals that accompany the material; b) video or audio training tapes; and c) training sessions or workshops. In addition, you may want to ask your supervisor if you can observe someone else teaching the program. Having a vision of what kinds of tasks the program includes, as well as how someone working with a group presents those tasks, keeps students engaged, and moves from task to task can be extremely valuable. It can also be useful to have regular problem-solving meetings with others who are using the program. For example, a teacher and three paraeducators who are all working with the same reading program may find that meeting every other week for 20 minutes to discuss concerns, ideas, and problems is both informative and comforting.

- **Review the instructional program to get a sense of the daily lessons and whether the format is consistent from day to day.**

Some instructional programs have daily consistency built into them and others do not. A remedial reading program entitled *Corrective Reading©* is an example of a consistent program. Each day's lesson consists of three major activities: word attack practice, group story reading, and individual student reading check-outs. The advantage of a consistent program is that once you learn the essentials of using that program, preparing for each day's lesson is very easy—all that's needed is a quick preview of the content to be covered.

In other programs, the components of the daily lesson may change from day to day. One day may involve a group art activity that requires arranging materials in advance, while the next day calls for having the group work together on a worksheet, and the third day's lesson consists of playing some kind of game. When a program has this degree of variety, learning the program will take longer and the preparation for each lesson will take more time.

- **Find out how much preparation time will be required for each lesson and when you are expected to prepare.**

As noted, when a program has a consistent lesson format, preparation time may be as little as five minutes and involve simply looking over the lesson for the next day. Non-consistent programs may require a full 15 minutes of preparation for each 30 minute lesson. If there is no preparation time built into your schedule, see if you can find creative ways to do lesson preparation during the group period. For example, if students work independently during a portion of the lesson, you might use a few minutes of that time to look over the lesson for the next day. Do not take away from one day's lesson to prepare for the next day, however. And if lack of preparation time is a problem, talk with your immediate and/or primary supervisor.

• **Find out about your responsibilities in terms of daily assignments or homework students are expected to complete.**

Monitoring and managing student work may be one of the most important responsibilities you have when doing small group work, and it is critical that you fully understand your supervising teacher's expectations regarding any assignments and/or homework. First you need to know whether or not students have daily assignments or homework that they are expected to complete. If they do, then you need to know when they are expected to complete the work, and where and when they are to turn in the work. Further, you need to ask the teacher what responsibility you have regarding correcting any assignments and homework. If you are supposed to correct the work, when are you to do that? Where do you find an answer key or some other guide to correcting and scoring? Are you to return the work to students? If so, when? Should students correct their errors and resubmit the work? Finally, you need to get information on any record keeping that you are expected to do for assignments and/or homework. If your supervisor does not have suggestions or preferences on these issues, you may want to ask about coming up with your own procedures which the supervisor can review.

• **Find out what supplies are generally needed to conduct a lesson, where you get them, and where you store them.**

With a consistent type of program, the supplies you will need (e.g., markers, pens, chalk) and the supplies students will need (e.g., pencils, pens, paper, bookmarks, folders for storing work or progress charts) are likely to be the same from day to day. In this case, you might ask your supervisor for tips on keeping things organized. In addition, find out from your supervisor what you should do if students who are expected to come to the group with their own supplies show up unprepared (e.g., what do you do if a student forgets to bring a pencil?). If supply needs will vary, ask your supervisor where you get necessary supplies and what procedures you should use to do so.

As you work with a group, you may figure out additional organizational strategies that will help the lesson run more smoothly. For example, you might assign some "housekeeping" jobs to students (one student passes out papers, one collects completed work, one distributes books). If you do this, be sure to rotate the jobs so that each student gets a turn to do each job. Also, you might want to keep your eye out for shelves, carts, boxes, baskets, clipboards, eraser boards and marking pens, and so on that are not being used but that may help support your work with the small group. Just remember not to take anything without asking first.

• **Find out what responsibilities you have, if any, in preparing for a substitute in the event you are not at school.**

First, you need to know whether someone else will teach your group if you are absent from school. If not, this question is irrelevant. If someone will be taking your place, however, ask your supervisor whether you should create some sort of Guest Teacher folder that contains all the essential information someone would need to work with the group. This would include some kind of lesson plan showing what lesson the students will be working on, what materials are needed, where those materials can be found, and instructions on assigning, collecting, grading, and recording student work. If preparing a

Guest Teacher folder is one of your expected responsibilities, wait until you have worked with the group for a week or two before you put the folder together. Then have your supervising teacher review it for clarity and completeness.

• **Find out whether the teacher has (and the students have been taught) any small group rules.**

Small group rules state the behaviors that students are expected to exhibit during a small group lesson. If your supervising teacher has rules, post them near where you work with your group. If your supervisor does not have rules, consider asking if you can design and post some of your own. Rules are useful because you can refer to them when you encourage responsible behavior or correct misbehavior (see Tasks 4 and 5 in this chapter). Figure 5.1 has some sample sets of rules:

• **Find out what kind of attention signal you should use during a small group lesson.**

An attention signal is used to get students to stop what they are doing and look at you. For

Figure 5.1

Sample Sets of Small Group Work Rules

PRIMARY LEVEL	INTERMEDIATE	MIDDLE SCHOOL/HIGH SCHOOL
Be ready to work.	Come prepared.	Come prepared with books, paper and pen/pencil, and any assignments or homework.
Listen.	Follow directions.	
Follow directions.	Do your best work.	Be in class, in seat, with materials out before the bell rings.
Keep hands and feet still and to yourself.	When you need help: wait your turn, stay seated, raise your hand, and be patient.	Stay on task (attention on the teacher, the board, or your own work).
		Persevere—if you don't get it at first, stick with it.
		When you need help: wait your turn, stay seated, raise your hand, and be patient.

example, if students have been working on a task with partners and it is time to move on to a different part of the lesson, you need some way to let students know to stop and look at you for the next directions. Ask your supervising teacher what kind of consistent signal you should use to get the attention of the small group. If your supervisor does not have one, you might ask if you could use something like the following: You raise one hand while saying, "Students, your attention please." Students are then taught that whenever you give that signal they should immediately stop whatever they are doing, raise their hand to signal others, and look at you with their mouth closed. (NOTE: If you work with middle or high school students, you may wish to modify the signal so that students do not raise their hands, but just quietly and politely prompt students around them to give their attention to you.)

- **Find out what, if any, housekeeping details you are expected to carry out and how.**

You need to know whether you are expected to get things ready for the group (e.g., arrange chairs, organize materials, and so on). More importantly, you need to know what procedures and materials you are to use in terms of monitoring attendance, including tardies. Once you understand these expectations, be very conscientious in implementing them so that the start of the lesson each day is consistent and predictable for the students. Don't wait to start the group until "stragglers" get there or you may find that more students start coming late.

- **Find out what procedures you are to use to prompt and reinforce responsible student behavior.**

Find out if your supervising teacher wants you to use any particular type of positive reinforcement strategies. Specifically, you need to know whether there is some kind of point system or token economy for rewarding positive behavior or whether you should ever use tangible rewards such as candy or cereal. In addition to any of these types of procedures that may be

requested by your supervisor, you need to provide frequent positive feedback to students. (NOTE: You will find more information on how to do this in Task 4 of this chapter.)

- **Find out what procedures you are to use when responding to student misbehavior.**

You need to know whether the teacher wants you to use any particular correction procedures and/or corrective consequences in response to misbehavior. Be sure to get detailed information on how to implement any procedure/consequence and any specific behavior(s) to use it with. (NOTE: Task 5 in this chapter provides information on responding to misbehavior that you may wish to discuss with your supervisor; however, be sure to use what your supervisor indicates.)

- **Find out what your responsibilities are in terms of communicating the behavioral expectations to students.**

Students need to know what is expected of them, just as you do. In many cases, your supervising teacher will have taught the expectations to the students before you start working with them. You may be expected to simply periodically review the expectations with students. In other cases, however, your supervisor will want you to teach students what the expectations are. You need to know what your responsibility is. In addition, you need to know how your supervisor wants you to teach and/or review the expectations. (NOTE: Task 3 in this chapter contains suggestions on teaching expectations, which you may wish to discuss with your supervisor.)

- **Find out what your responsibilities are in terms of giving your supervising teacher feedback on the students' academic and/or behavioral performance.**

Your job is to support instruction—it is your supervising teacher who shoulders responsibility for making instructional decisions about students. Therefore, an important part of working with a small group is to keep your supervisor informed of student progress. To do so, you need to know exactly what kind of information your supervisor wants and in what form he or she wants it. You also need to know how frequently he or she expects to hear from you (daily, weekly, or only if one or more students are having trouble), and when the two of you can meet to discuss the feedback. For example, your supervisor may have you keep records on students' reading rates, error rates, scores on worksheets or other assignments, and so on. This information must be accurate and collected with whatever regularity the teacher needs it to be, to make decisions. For students who have an IEP, this information will be used to make decisions about whether or not each student's goals are being met. Be sure to get specific details from your supervising teacher about collecting and sharing feedback on students.

In addition to responding to your supervisor's expectations, you might want to consider keeping a spiral binder (or anything else that works for you) in which you can make notes on things you need to get ready for the next lesson. For example, if during a lesson you notice that one of the students' books has pages missing, you might write in your binder, "Todd's CRP book is missing pages 112-115. Get a new book or copy those pages." This is the kind of thing that you are likely to forget by the end of the day, but will take care of if you made a note of it at the time. You can also make notes regarding things you want to discuss with the teacher at your next meeting time. For example, you might note, "Charlesa seems kind of quiet and discouraged. Should I be doing anything differently to help her?"

Small Group Work: Procedures and Expectations

Small Group: _____

Supervisor: _____ Schedule: _____

1. What time does the group begin and what time does it end?

2. What are my responsibilities in terms of getting students to the group? from the group?

3. What instructional materials will I be using? How will I be trained to use the materials effectively?

4. How much preparation time is required to get ready for each lesson? When do I do that preparation (right before the scheduled group time, right after to prepare for the next day, at the end of the day)?

5. What are the procedures and what are my responsibilities in terms of students' daily assignments and/or homework?

6. What supplies will I need each day? What supplies will students need each day? Where do I get the supplies and where do I store them?

7. What are my responsibilities in preparing for a substitute in the event I am not at school?

8. What small group rules am I expected to use?

9. How do I signal students that I need their attention?

10. What are my "housekeeping" responsibilities (getting ready; attendance, etc.)?

11. What procedures do you want me to use to prompt and reinforce responsible behavior?

12. What procedures do you want me to use for correcting misbehavior?

13. What is my responsibility in terms of communicating the behavioral expectations to students? How am I to teach and/or review the expectations?

14. What exactly are my responsibilities in terms of providing feedback on student performance?

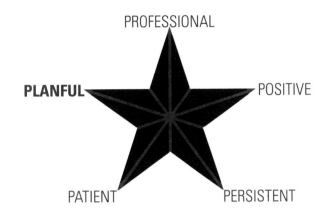

PROFESSIONAL

PLANFUL — POSITIVE

PATIENT   PERSISTENT

TASK 2:

Know the behavioral expectations for students.

To successfully work with a small group, you need to know in advance exactly what the teacher expects student behavior to be like during the small group period. When you are certain how students are expected to behave, you can make immediate and effective decisions while you are working with the group about when to praise responsible behavior and when/how to correct misbehavior. If you don't know what student behavior should look and sound like, you will have no basis for determining whether students are exhibiting responsible behavior or irresponsible behavior.

Determining expectations for small group work can be tricky because there are often several different activities that occur within one lesson, and each may involve different expectations for student behavior. For example, if you were working with a small group using the *Corrective Reading©* program presented in Task 1, each daily lesson would consist of the following activities:

Word attack practice

Group story reading

Individual reading check-outs

Thus, you would need to know, in detail, what behaviors are to be encouraged and what behaviors are to be corrected for each of those three activities.

During the group story reading activity in which students in the group take turns reading sentences in the story, you would need to know whether students are expected to follow along with their finger so that you can tell that they are reading. If your supervisor's expectation is that students follow along, then not doing so would be a minor misbehavior that should be corrected. On the other hand, if your supervisor doesn't care whether or not students follow along, then you wouldn't bother to correct them if they are not. (See Task 5 in this chapter for more information on how to correct misbehavior.)

The point is, you need to know EXACTLY what the teacher wants for each different activity or type of activity that will occur during a lesson. Instead of a "How To Do It" section for this

WHEN YOU KNOW WHAT BEHAVIORS ARE EXPECTED OF STUDENTS, YOU CAN QUICKLY DETERMINE WHETHER YOU SHOULD BE PRAISING OR CORRECTING THEIR BEHAVIOR.

In addition to knowing the expectations for each of the lesson's activities, you also need to find out your supervisor's expectations for student behavior during the transitions that precede and follow each major activity. To identify the transitions that might occur during your small group time and what they might involve, start by creating a schedule of the daily lesson activities. Then figure out what is required of students to get from one activity to the next and how long it should take. Ask your supervising teacher to help you. See the example in Figure 5.4. The left-hand column lists the daily activities of a *Corrective Reading©* lesson and the right-hand column contains a detailed example of transition expectations.

task, we have included a reproducible worksheet (Figure 5.3), titled "CHAMPs Expectations for Students During Small Group." This worksheet uses the acronym CHAMPs, to prompt you to find out the details of the teacher's expectations for Conversation, Help, Activity, Movement, and Participation. (Depending on the instructional program, the Activity may or may not vary from day to day.) We recommend that you reproduce and complete one of these worksheets for each of the major activities that are likely to occur during the daily lessons of your small group. Thus, for the *Corrective Reading©* example, you would complete three of these sheets: one for word attack practice, one for group story reading, and one for individual check-outs.

Use the CHAMPs worksheet to guide your discussion with your supervisor regarding his/her expectations for student behavior during each of the different activities. Try to arrange time with your supervising teacher before the first day you are to start this responsibility. Say something like, "Mrs. Pulanski, before I start working with the small group I would like to find out what you want me to be doing. May I ask you some questions about how I can be of assistance?"

Inefficient transitions from one activity to another can wipe out precious instructional time.

CHAMPs Expectations for Students During Small Group

Group: _____

Supervisor: _____ Schedule: _____

CONVERSATION

Can students engage in conversations with each other during this activity?

If yes, about what?

With whom can they speak (how far away)?

How many students can be involved in a single conversation?

How long can the conversation last?

HELP

How do students get questions answered? How do students get your attention?

What should they do while they are waiting?

If the teacher is in the room, and a student asks permission to speak to him/her, is that acceptable or not?

ACTIVITY

What is the type of activity (direct teaching-question/answer, group work, independent work, pair practice? (NOTE: This may vary from day to day.)

MOVEMENT

Can students get out of their seats (leave the group) during this activity?

If yes, acceptable reasons include:

Pencil   Restroom

Drink   Hand in/pick up materials

Other:

Do they need permission?

PARTICIPATION

What behaviors show that students are participating fully and responsibly in this part of the lesson?

What behaviors show that a student is not participating?

Figure 5.4

LESSON ACTIVITIES	TRANSITION EXPECTATIONS
	Students enter the room, pick up their packet, and should be in seat and ready for group before the bell rings. They can talk quietly until the bell rings and during the time attendance is being taken.
WORD ATTACK AT BOARD	
	Students should focus attention from top of story sheet to lower on the page where the story begins. This should take no more than five seconds.
WORD ATTACK ON STORY SHEETS	
	Students should open their books to the correct page to get ready for Word Attack on story sheets. This should take no more than 15 seconds.
GROUP STORY READING	
	Students move from the small group area to classroom desks, and should begin studying the story to get ready for check-out. Some talking during this transition is fine, but when given the instruction, "Get ready for check-outs, please" talking will cease. This should require no more than 30 seconds.

After you have worked with a small group for awhile, you may feel that the lessons would be more effective if the expectations were different. For example, the teacher may allow students to stand during individual reading check-outs, and you think they should remain seated. If you choose to ask your supervisor's opinion about modifying the expectations, be careful to present your suggestion(s) in a skillful manner. Remember, it is your supervisor's responsibility to make all final decisions about expectations for student behavior and your responsibility to carry out those decisions.

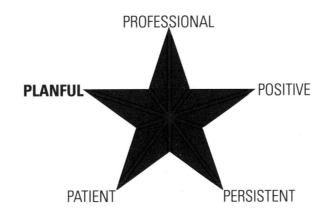

TASK 3:

Teach the behavioral expectations to students (as needed).

In addition to knowing the teacher's expectations for student behavior, you need to know what is expected of you in terms of communicating those expectations to students. In some cases, your supervisor may have taught or may plan to teach the expectations to students—and will only want you to review the expectations with students. In other cases, your supervisor will want you to actually teach the expectations yourself. This task presents information and suggestions on how to teach expectations.

Communicating expectations to students is critical to managing behavior effectively. If the behavioral expectations have not been shared with students, some students will misbehave simply because they don't know what is expected. For example, a student may talk to another student during some part of the lesson just because she did not know that talking was not acceptable at that point in the lesson. In addition, when expectations are not taught, some students will test, or experiment with, different

behaviors to see what will be tolerated. Effectively teaching the expectations allows you to be very specific with students about what responsible and irresponsible behavior should look like and sound like in all major parts of a lesson and during the transitions between various parts of the lesson. Thus, the content for teaching expectations comes from the information on Conversation, Help, Activity, Movement, and Participation that you have summarized on the CHAMPs form(s)—see Task 2 of this chapter.

The "How To Do It" section of this task offers some basic guidelines for teaching expectations and some specific teaching strategies. As always, you should review this information with your supervising teacher before implementing any of the suggestions.

HOW TO DO IT:

- **Set up a schedule for teaching expectations.**

Plan to teach the expectations every day for the first three to five days that you work with a small group. The lessons do not need to be long, and they should occur close to the activity itself. For example, you might initially take two or three minutes immediately before each major lesson activity to teach the expectations for that activity. After several days of instruction, if students seem to know the expectations and actually meet those expectations, you might have students move directly from one part of the lesson to the next. However, if students seem at all unsure what is expected or if there is a lot of misbehavior during the work period, continue conducting short lessons, using one or more of the strategies that follow. Also you should plan to reteach the lessons just before and for at least two consecutive days after major vacations.

Remember, you need lessons for each major activity and transition that will occur during your small group work period.

• Use a variety of teaching strategies to maintain student attention.

Using different strategies to teach the same content over several days will make reviewing the content less boring for students. Following is a list of various strategies for teaching expectations. For each strategy there is a brief description, including tips on the age-appropriateness of the strategy.

—Describe the expectations.

This involves simply telling students what is expected of them and is probably the least effective strategy for teaching expectations initially. That is because many students simply tune out a "lecture." By the fourth or fifth day, however, you may wish to use this as a quick review. "Students, remember that during the Word Attack portion of the lesson you should . . . ." Even as a review, do not use this with young children (preschool through third grade). Young children pay attention better to visuals, demonstrations, and role plays.

—Use a completed CHAMPs worksheet on an overhead projector.

Make a transparency of the CHAMPs worksheet (see Task 2) for each lesson activity and

transition, and fill in your expectations in large print. Put the transparency on an overhead projector as you teach students your expectations. Figure 5.5, CHAMPs worksheet as an overhead transparency, shows what this might look like (although your expectations may be different). This is an appropriate technique as long as the students have adequate reading skills. Therefore it would not be advisable for students in preschool, kindergarten, or early first grade, or with older students who have extremely poor reading skills.

Figure 5.5 CHAMPs Transparency

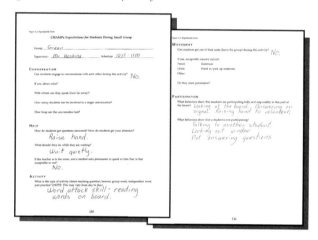

—Use a "Looks like/ Sounds like T-chart."

On a poster or a transparency make a chart like the one in Figure 5.6 (although obviously the content will reflect your and your supervisor's expectations). It is called a T-chart because the lines forming the sections of the chart look like an upper-case T. A T-chart is an easy way to provide very specific information about what student behavior should look like and sound like. If done on a poster, you can leave it on the wall as an ongoing reminder to students. T-charts are effective with any age group; however, with non-readers use pictures or graphics instead of text.

—Display positive expectations in a notebook.

If you go to many different locations, it may not be possible to use posters or transparencies. An alternative is a three-ring binder in which

140

Figure 5.6 Sample T-Chart

Word Attack

WORD ATTACK LOOKS LIKE:	WORD ATTACK SOUNDS LIKE:
Eyes on the board or your paper.	Everyone's voice together on signal.
Sitting tall, hands and feet still.	No one answers before or after the signal.
Raise your hand if you have a question.	During individual turns, only one student talking, everyone else listening.
Everyone working together as a group.	

you have one-page displays of your expectations for various activities. You can take the binder with you from class to class and prop it open so it looks like a small tent. (See Figure 5.7). Use tabs to label each page so you can easily flip to the appropriate expectations for each different activity for each different group. When you actually teach your expectations, place the notebook in a prominent position where students can see it (e.g., on top of a file cabinet). A major advantage of this strategy is that you can

easily display your expectations every day, not just during the first five "teaching" days. This strategy is probably most appropriate for use in grades three through eight, although it could be used with younger students if the displays used pictures or graphics.

—Demonstrate the expectations.

Demonstrating expectations is very effective because, rather than just telling students what active participation looks and sounds like, you show them. That is, you act out the positive expectations you have for students. You might also demonstrate the kinds of behaviors you don't want to see (e.g. staring out the window or tapping a pencil). When modeling a negative behavior, it can be useful to be somewhat humorous, but be sure it does not seem as if you are making fun of the students. Also, if you choose to demonstrate a negative behavior, always model the positive expectation both before and after the negative example. Demonstrations are appropriate with any age students.

— Have several students demonstrate correctly meeting the expectation.

Figure 5.7 Sample Expectations Notebook

Group Story Reading

• Follow along with your finger so you are ready when it is your turn.

• Raise your hand if you hear a mistake, but say nothing until called on.

• Use a strong, confident voice when you read.

On the second or third day of teaching your expectations, you might call on volunteers to demonstrate the right way to meet the expectation. Do not have students act out negative behaviors. This procedure is best with students in preschool through fourth grade.

—*Have all students practice the positive expectations.*

Once you have demonstrated how to exhibit the positive expectations, have everyone in the class demonstrate how to do it. For example, after showing students how they are to get your attention if they have a question, you might say, "Everyone show me what you will do if you have a question and you want me to call on you. That's right, everyone quietly raised their hand. Now show me what it looks like to . . . ." This technique is especially useful with students in preschool through fourth grade.

—*Have students identify whether you are demonstrating the expectation or not.*

A good way to review expectations is to model different behaviors and have students tell you whether each behavior modeled is the right way or the wrong way to behave. "Watch me. Raise your hand when you can tell me whether I am being on-task or off-task when we do board work."

—*Review the expectations by asking questions.*

Another good way to review expectations after they have been taught for a couple of days is to ask students direct questions about expectations. "Everyone, get ready to tell me one reason you can get out of your seat without permission." If you use this strategy, call on students randomly rather than asking for volunteers. This increases the chance that every student will think about the question. Simply tell students that you are going to ask the question, give everyone time to think about the correct answer, and then call on one individual. This technique can be used with all grade levels.

142

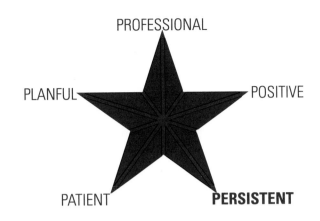

PROFESSIONAL

PLANFUL   POSITIVE

PATIENT   **PERSISTENT**

TASK 4:

Use effective instructional techniques.

*W*hen part of your job entails supporting instruction by working with a small group (or groups), you should be aware of effective instructional techniques. This task presents information on four major variables that positively affect instruction. These include: a) incorporating all the components of a well-structured daily lesson; b) keeping students' attention focused on the lesson; c) responding appropriately to students' correct answers (verbal and written); and d) responding appropriately to students' incorrect answers (verbal and written).

The "Persistent" point of the star is highlighted because working with small groups requires presenting and representing the material until students successfully demonstrate they understand the essential skills and concepts. Just like good coaching in sports, small group work involves demonstrations, repetition, practice, and repetition. When you are persistent (and patient), the students will learn that you have high expectations and will do whatever is necessary to help them learn.

HOW TO DO IT:

- **Be aware of the components of an effective lesson.**

If you work with a small group, you are likely to use an instructional program (i.e., a curriculum) that specifies the tasks and activities that make up the daily lessons for that group. Understanding the sequence of activities that comprises an effective lesson can help you implement a curriculum more successfully. The information can also be useful should you need to prepare lessons yourself (e.g., the program does not provide structured daily lessons). Following are brief descriptions of the components of a well-structured lesson.

—Start with a review of previously taught skills or concepts.

Regular review of known information helps students retain that information over time. If the content from previous lessons is never reviewed (or referred to), students are likely to assume that they only have to retain what is taught until the end of a lesson, and not think about it again. Reviewing previously learned information reinforces the knowledge gained and demonstrates that what has been learned is important. A review can be as short as a couple of minutes or as long as one-third of the lesson. It can (and should) be structured in a variety of ways—for example, as a presentation/discussion, a question/answer session, or a short quiz.

—Preview what is to be learned in the lesson.

Before actually starting with any new content, take one to two minutes to tell students where the lesson is headed and why the content is important or useful. This is sometimes referred to as "sharing lesson objectives with the students." It's important that students realize that each lesson has a purpose and that you will help them successfully achieve that purpose. When students don't know what they will be learning and why, they are more likely to perceive certain information or activities as nothing more than "busywork" just to keep them occupied. As you tell students where the lesson is going, relate the new knowledge to previous content. This not only prepares students to be active learners of the new information, but also helps them see the value of previously learned content.

—Provide instruction on new skills or concepts.

"Providing instruction" includes communicating the information, skills, or concepts to students and leading them through practice opportunities until they can demonstrate mastery of the material. Initially, you want to tell students the information and, whenever possible, demonstrate or model how to do it. Say, for example, you are working with a math group. After briefly reviewing recently learned concepts and sharing the objectives for the day, you might explain how to do a new type of problem and then have students watch as you do a couple of problems on the board or an overhead projector. You would then lead or guide students as together you work several more problems. "How do we start this problem? Right. Who can tell me what we would do next? Yes, Margaret. Who can tell me what we would do after that?"

If a skill or concept is particularly complex or lengthy, consider breaking it down into component parts or steps. Model and lead the group through the first step of several problems. Then model and lead students through the second step. After demonstrating how to do the first and second steps together, have students complete both steps on two or three problems. As each new step is introduced, add it to the previous steps, until the entire process/concept is completed. It's important during a lesson to make sure that students have non-threatening practice opportunities. Leading students through problems provides non-threatening practice for them and the chance for you to give them any needed feedback. Structure your lessons in such a way that students know it is okay to make mistakes, and that when they do make mistakes you will help them.

—Assess student understanding of material taught.

Once you have led students through several sample problems/questions, have the students do some problems/questions without your assistance. This is how you can determine whether or not they have reached mastery. When they can correctly do the work, you can introduce another new concept. If students cannot successfully demonstrate mastery, continue modeling and leading until they are proficient with the concept or skill. Once students have demonstrated mastery, you can assign independent work. Usually this means giving students an assignment that they work on independently or in cooperative groups.

• During small group work, maintain student attention on the lesson.

Keeping the students' attention focused on the lesson is critical if they are going to learn the material. Think about a teacher you had who "captured" students' attention and made learning fun. Class time probably flew by. Now think about a teacher who had no passion or enthusiasm, who never got students involved. Class time probably dragged on forever. Your students will learn more when you can make the lessons as informative and interesting as possible. Following are suggestions for ways you can keep students interested in the lessons you present.

—Follow the 20-minute rule.

Avoid having students (especially young students) engage in any single type of activity for more than

20 minutes. An activity that students are expected to do for longer than 20 minutes is likely to result in a loss of student attention. So, if you have been demonstrating problems for 10 minutes, stop and assign some problems for the students to work on independently for five minutes. Then have them work in partners for three minutes. At that point you can pull the group back together and demonstrate some different types of problems.

—Maintain instructional momentum.

This means that you keep things moving. It is easier for students to keep focused on a lesson when the content/activity occupies their minds. When a lesson is too slow or seems boring (because nothing is happening), students will begin to think about things other than the lesson and you will have lost their attention. There are a number of ways you can maintain instructional momentum.

—Act like you are interested in what you are presenting.

If you act bored, so will the students. On the other hand, your enthusiasm will be catching.

—Don't talk too much.

Students will pay less attention to a lesson that does not actively involve them, so don't just lecture. Ask questions and present things for students to do. You might want to consider using group choral responses for practice opportunities. For example, if part of the lesson involves having students practice reading word lists, have all the students read the list together after you signal them to respond. (NOTE: If your immediate supervisor uses group responses, you might ask to observe how to implement this technique.)

—Incorporate variety in your presentation.

You can vary the pace—sometimes speaking quickly, sometimes slowing down. You can vary the volume of your delivery. You can even vary the emotional intensity of the lesson—sometimes making it important and intense, then a few minutes later making it relaxed and easy.

—Use humor.

Laughter makes learning more fun and makes it easier for students to pay attention.

• *For a particularly difficult or undesirable task, increase your enthusiasm.*

If you know there's a part of the lesson that students don't like, act like you are looking forward to it because you know the students will be able to be successful. Your enthusiasm and optimism will help reduce the students' concerns and complaints.

• *Use "change-ups" when a lesson starts to lag.*

A "change-up" is anything that gives students a brief break and helps to freshen their attention. For example, if you are working with primary students who are beginning to show signs of restlessness, you might stop the lesson and play a 30-second game of "Simon Says" to get them out of their seats and give them practice following a quick but fun sequence of instructions. Older students often enjoy tackling a mental puzzle or "brainteaser." You can find books of mental games in most bookstores.

• **Reinforce students for correct responses and for making progress.**

As you work with a small group, provide frequent confirmation of students' correct verbal and written responses. When first learning something new, students will not know whether they understand the concept or are doing the procedure correctly. You can easily confirm their efforts with short and simple statements such as, "Yes," or "Correct", or "Right." With a particularly difficult concept or step, you might confirm by reiterating the important information. "Yes, everyone remembered to carry the two tens over to the tens column." Make your confirmations of correct responses short enough that they feel like a natural part of the lesson. In the early stages of learning a skill or concept, try to confirm every response. As students become more familiar and comfortable with the concept/process (i.e., they are rarely making mistakes), confirmations can be more intermittent (e.g., you might confirm one out of every three to ten correct responses rather than every response).

In addition to confirmation of correct responses, acknowledge any significant progress made by the group or by individuals. For example, if a group had trouble mastering a particular math skill, but on the last assignment everyone did well, let the students know. "On yesterday's assignment no one made a single error on the regrouping problems. That gave us some trouble for a few days, but each of you kept trying, you paid attention in class, and now you've got it. We are going to keep practicing this type of problem, but each of you should be proud of your perseverance. Perseverance means you stick with something until you get it!" Notice that this is longer than a simple confirmation. It is more like a minor celebration of an important learning milestone.

- **Correct incorrect student responses in a way that helps students learn the material.**

The goal of corrections is to reduce the likelihood that the student(s) will make the same error in the future. Some people think that the most positive thing you can do is ignore errors so that students don't get discouraged. This is not a positive thing to do. If you don't correct mistakes, students cannot learn from their errors. What you want to do is correct student errors supportively. When a student makes an error, correct it as quickly as possible. Provide information and have the student do the task (or answer the question) again until he or she can do it successfully. The longer the time between the error and the correction, the less effective the correction will be in helping the student learn from the mistake.

In general, correction procedures for content errors consist of providing the information students need in order to perform the task successfully. If the error involves a simple fact, state the fact. "The Bill of Rights is actually the first ten amendments to the Constitution." If the error involves a process or operation, review the process or steps for arriving at the correct response. "Remember that when there is an e at the end of a word, it will make this letter say its name. What is the name of this letter? Yes, o. So what is the word? Right, rope."

Avoid corrections that take too long or try to "drag" information out of the student. For example, avoid statements like, "I know you can do this. Look at it again. You did problems like these yesterday, so I know you know how. Just think." Nothing in the preceding correction will help a student get the correct response. However, it is likely to put a lot of pressure on the student and may leave the student feeling stupid if she cannot respond correctly.

When students are first learning a new concept or skill, monitor their performance closely so that you can catch error patterns early. If students are allowed to do a whole series of problems wrong, they end up practicing their error(s)—and practice makes perfect. If you notice that half the students in your group make errors on the first three problems of an assignment, for example, bring the students back together and complete the first half of the assignment as a group.

When you know the content well (e.g., you have taught it before), you can precorrect high probability errors. For example, if you know that students often make errors when reading silent e words, you can correct the error before students even have an opportunity to make the mistake. "Before you read the next word, see whether there is an e at the end of the word. Think about what that e does to the sound of this letter. Now tell me, what is this word?"

Remember that making errors can be anxiety producing and discouraging for students. If your students are making lots of errors, praise them for their hard work and perseverance. You might say something like, "This is a really tough kind of problem, but you will get it." Keep praise, correct response confirmations, guided practice, and precorrections at a very high level until students have mastered a difficult skill or concept. This could take a few minutes or it could take a few weeks. Once students have demonstrated mastery, be sure to congratulate the group for successfully achieving this difficult milestone in their learning.

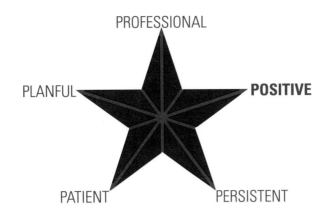

PROFESSIONAL

PLANFUL

POSITIVE

PATIENT

PERSISTENT

TASK 5:

Manage student behavior effectively.

Effective instruction is just about impossible without responsible student behavior. This task addresses how to effectively manage student behavior when working with a small group. Information is provided on how to monitor group behavior, how to prompt the desired behaviors, how to provide positive feedback during and after the small group worktime, and how to deal with misbehavior that is likely to occur.

We have highlighted the "Positive" point of the star because managing student behavior effectively allows you to set a positive tone, which in turn will keep misbehavior to a minimum, encourage responsible behavior, and communicate that learning is worthwhile and fun.

HOW TO DO IT:

• Use visual scanning to monitor student activity.

Maintaining frequent eye contact is essential when working with a small group. Not only does it let the students know that there will be no opportunity to "get away" with anything, but

it allows you to show students that when they behave responsibly you will notice. Scanning means looking at students frequently, regardless of what you are doing. When you are doing boardwork, you obviously have to look at the board, but you also need to make a point of looking at the students. In fact, your goal should be to look at the students more than you look at the board. If you are doing an activity like group story reading, where individual students take turns reading sentences, you need to look at the student who is reading and track the text in your own book to monitor the accuracy of the student's reading. You also need to periodically glance at the other students to see that they are following along and behaving responsibly. Doing many things at once can be difficult, but it gets easier with practice.

In order to be able to scan, you need to make sure that the physical layout of the small group gives you a direct line of sight to all students at all times. Don't allow any students to pull back from the group so you can't see what they are doing. Also, keep in mind that it is easy to focus on the students in the middle of the group and forget about the students on the edges-and it is often the students getting the least eye contact from you who will tend to exhibit irresponsible behavior. Therefore, make a conscious effort to look more frequently at the edges of your group. Finally, if you do have a student on the edge of the group who misbehaves, move that student to the middle and place a more responsible student on the end.

• Prompt responsible student behavior.

Prompts are quick reminders or instructions that will help keep everyone in the group together and on-task. "Everyone, put your finger on the first word of the sentence. Kenchi, please read that sentence while everyone else follows along. Remember, raise your hand if you hear an error." Including prompts as part of the flow of your instruction helps students know what is expected and what is supposed to be happening during various points in the lesson. Prompts can also be used to let students know about time constraints or upcoming transitions. "You have about one minute left to finish that part of the task, then we start checkouts." Following are some common prompts that might be useful in small group instruction.

—*You should be quietly reading the story while we are waiting for others to arrive.*

—*Eyes up here, it is time to begin.*

—*Answer when I give the signal.*

—***Get your books and pencil out. Please keep your book closed until I tell you which page we are working on.***

—*Everyone look at the board.*

—*Hands and feet still.*

—***Keep your attention focused on the sentence*** *you are reading.*

—*Two minutes left to finish up and get ready to leave.*

Prompts can also be used to prevent predictable problems. For example, say students frequently have trouble keeping track of where they are during the group story reading, so you end up spending time helping them find their places. Immediately before story reading, you might give a detailed prompt to clarify your expectations. "Students, today during story reading remember to follow along. Pay careful attention to the person reading. Don't let anything distract you or make you lose your place. That way when I call on you, you will know exactly where we are without needing me to nag or remind you."

• Reinforce responsible student behavior.

You want to reinforce students when they are meeting the expectations for responsible behavior during small group work. You can do this by providing positive feedback in a manner that does not interrupt the flow of the lesson, yet lets students know how well they are doing. There are three major types of positive feedback that you want to give students during small group work. The first has to do with letting students know that their verbal and written responses are correct. This type of feedback is covered in Task 4 of this chapter. The second type of positive feedback has to do with reinforcing an entire group for its behavior, and the third has to do with reinforcing

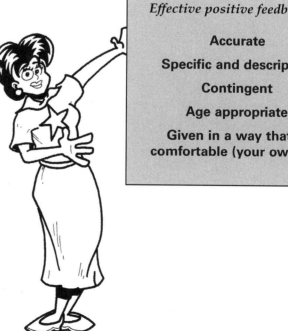

Effective positive feedback is:

Accurate

Specific and descriptive

Contingent

Age appropriate

Given in a way that is comfortable (your own style)

individual students regarding their individual behavior.

When everyone in a group is behaving responsibly, praise the group. "Everyone is doing a fine job of staying focused and answering together on signal." This type of feedback is useful and efficient because in one statement you let everyone in the group know that they are meeting the behavioral expectations for that portion of the lesson. It also creates a sense of "groupness" that can help students begin to take pride in the group's, not just their own, behavior. The most important thing to keep in mind regarding group feedback is that you should not use it unless EVERYONE in the group is meeting expectations. A statement like, "Almost everyone is . . ." only turns students' attention from the task at hand to wondering who isn't meeting expectations. Use group feedback during a lesson and at the end of the group time if it was an especially good day. "Today was great. Everybody followed the rules, was supportive of others in the group, and kept their attention focused. I hope we have more days just like this."

Group praise, however, is not terribly reinforcing to individual students. For example, think about when your principal compliments the entire staff. It's nice to hear, but not necessarily very meaningful to you personally. Contrast that to the principal observing your work with a small group and then complimenting you on your clear instruction and wonderful ability to keep students engaged. For most people, an individual compliment is more powerful than a group compliment.

When praising individual students, keep it very brief. "Deon, nice job of getting started on those problems." Think of positive feedback as a sort of subtext within instruction. The main text will always be the instructional content or information, but periodically there can be an "aside" on the positive behavior of one or more individuals.

When thinking about how much positive feedback to give, consider the amount of misbehavior you generally have to correct and remember the concept of a 3 to 1 ratio of positive interactions to negative interactions (see Chapter 3, Task 5). The more you are correcting misbehavior, the more frequently you should be giving positive feedback. On the other hand, if a group works very well with very little misbehavior, less positive feedback is needed. Now, it's not that the well-behaved group of students doesn't need or deserve any positive feedback—they just don't need as much of it. This may seem counterintuitive because most adults tend to lavish praise on a well-behaved group and nag and scold a problem group. However, students in a problem group, because of their misbehavior, usually get a lot less positive feedback. You need to search for and comment on their responsible behavior frequently. If you do, the behavior will soon improve. Don't forget the importance of non-contingent acknowledgement for students as well. Greeting students when they enter the room, saying "hello" when you see them in the hall, asking how they are doing-all demonstrate to students that you care about them.

If your supervising teacher uses (and wants you to use) a point or token system to reinforce responsible behavior, find out if you are supposed to award the points/tokens throughout the lesson or only at the end. Also, watch out for the tendency to "play favorites" by giving more points to the students you like and less to those you don't. Always award points objectively, based on the actual behavior of the students on that day. Do not let yourself hold any sort of grudge based on misbehavior from previous days.

• Effectively respond to student misbehavior.

When responding to misbehavior that occurs during small group work, don't forget the basics introduced in Chapter 3. That is, remember to be: a) patient and calm; b) persistent and consistent; and c) professional (i.e., don't take the behavior personally, and think before you respond). Also remember to be planful about how you will respond. That is, anticipate the misbehaviors that are likely to occur and know exactly what you will do if they occur.

In addition to those basic concepts, you might also want to keep the following specific tips in mind:

—*Intervene as soon as you observe the misbehavior.*

Do not let a misbehavior go on because it will usually get worse and be harder to correct later.

—*Try a verbal correction first.*

Look at the student (or students) engaged in misbehavior and state what the student should be doing. "Tina, you should have your feet on the floor and your hands in your lap."

—*Try praising students who are doing what the misbehaving student(s) should be doing.*

You might say something like, "Vern and Rico are being very responsible; they are keeping their eyes on the book and answering every question." This is particularly effective with students in the primary grades.

—*If a misbehavior continues, calmly and consistently implement a corrective consequence.*

Remember, don't argue with the student(s). Simply state the misbehavior and the consequence. If the student argues with you, restate the expectation. Later, discuss the problem with your supervisor. (For additional ideas on dealing with power struggles, See Chapter 3, Task 7.)

Following are brief descriptions of corrective consequences that are both effective and appropriate for use during small group work. You may wish to discuss this information with your supervisor, but remember that it is your supervisor's job to make decisions about the consequences you actually will use.

—*Time-out from small group*

If a student continues to misbehave, even after a reprimand, have the student push his chair back so that he is not at the table (or in the semicircle of chairs). After about two minutes tell the student to rejoin the group.

—*Time-out area*

This consequence requires that a time-out area, which can be as simple as a chair in a low traffic area of the classroom, has already been set up in the classroom. The maximum length of time a student should be assigned for time-out is three minutes with primary students (grades K-3) and five minutes with older students. A student sent to time-out should have nothing to do, and should be held accountable for completing any written work that was assigned while the student was in time-out.

—*Demerits*

Demerits are essentially negative points which, when accumulated, lead to a more severe consequence. In a middle school resource room, for example, it might be that each time you have to remind a student to get back to work, the student receives one demerit. If a student gets more than three demerits in one class period, that student is assigned to an after-school detention. Implementing this consequence requires some kind of system to keep track of demerits.

—Point fines

Point fines can only be used if the supervising teacher has implemented a positive reinforcement point system. If there is such a system in place, the teacher may tell you that for each infraction a student commits, that student loses one point. As with demerits, some kind of tracking system is required.

—Time-owed

Time-owed involves taking away a small amount of time (e.g., one minute) from an activity such as recess for each infraction a student commits. Do not use this consequence unless instructed to do so by your supervising teacher. The teacher has to ensure that there is some way to supervise those students who owe time. If it is an acceptable consequence, you might have middle school or high school students owe 15 seconds off the next passing period for each infraction.

—Change in seat

If two students have trouble staying on task when they sit together, do not let them sit together. If possible, make sure there are at least two responsible students between the individuals who engaged in the misbehavior. After a few days, if the two students demonstrate responsible behavior, you can give them the chance to sit next to each other again.

If one individual misbehaves for several days, you might have that student sit right next to you during the group time. If the behavior improves, you can try moving the student back to the original seat.

CHAPTER 5 ACTIVITIES

THINK ABOUT IT

Use the following chart to evaluate your familiarity with the material presented in this chapter. When you have completed this activity, enter reminders about the tasks you wanted to reread or discuss into your planning calendar.

Figure 5.8 Reproducible Form

	The information was not applicable to my situation.	The information was familiar. I consistently implement the strategies presented.	The information was useful. I should reread this task at least once more this year.	Some of the information was new. I should reread this task within a month.	Much of the information was new. I should discuss it with my supervisor or with other paraeducators.
TASK 1: Know the procedures, materials, and what is expected of you.	0	1	2	3	4
TASK 2: Know the behavioral expectations for students.	0	1	2	3	4
TASK 3: Teach the behavioral expectations to students (as needed).	0	1	2	3	4
TASK 4: Use effective instructional techniques.	0	1	2	3	4
TASK 5: Manage student behavior effectively.	0	1	2	3	4

(NOTE: On pages 205-210, in the back of the book, you will find a complete chart of all the tasks in the book. You may wish to summarize the information from each individual chapter on this single chart.)

TAKE ACTION

For one day, monitor the degree to which student behavior in your small group matches the CHAMPs expectations you have identified for that group (see Task 2). The CHAMPs Expectations v. Reality forms in Figures 5.8 and 5.9 allow you to rate student behavior on the following scale:

5 = All students met expectations

4 = All but one or two students met expectations

3 = Most students met expectations

2 = About half the class met expectations

1 = Most students did not meet expectations

Please note that on the first page of the form the "Activity" section has been filled in with the following activities: Coming to group, Teacher directed work, Cooperative group work, Independent work, Wrap-up and leave. These activities may or may not be applicable to your small group. Therefore, on the second page of the form, the "Activity" sections are blank so that you can fill in activities appropriate to your own small group.

CHAMPs Expectations v. Reality Rating Sheet

CONVERSATION	1 2 3 4 5
HELP (Teacher Attention)	1 2 3 4 5
ACTIVITY *Coming to group*	
MOVEMENT	1 2 3 4 5
PARTICIPATION	1 2 3 4 5
CONVERSATION	1 2 3 4 5

CONVERSATION	1 2 3 4 5
HELP (Teacher Attention)	1 2 3 4 5
ACTIVITY *Tchr. Directed Wk.*	
MOVEMENT	1 2 3 4 5
PARTICIPATION	1 2 3 4 5
CONVERSATION	1 2 3 4 5

CONVERSATION	1 2 3 4 5
HELP (Teacher Attention)	1 2 3 4 5
ACTIVITY *Coop. Grp. Wk.*	
MOVEMENT	1 2 3 4 5
PARTICIPATION	1 2 3 4 5
CONVERSATION	1 2 3 4 5

CONVERSATION	1 2 3 4 5
HELP (Teacher Attention)	1 2 3 4 5
ACTIVITY *Independent Wk.*	
MOVEMENT	1 2 3 4 5
PARTICIPATION	1 2 3 4 5
CONVERSATION	1 2 3 4 5

CONVERSATION	1 2 3 4 5
HELP (Teacher Attention)	1 2 3 4 5
ACTIVITY *Wrap-up & leave*	
MOVEMENT	1 2 3 4 5
PARTICIPATION	1 2 3 4 5
CONVERSATION	1 2 3 4 5

CONVERSATION	1 2 3 4 5
HELP (Teacher Attention)	1 2 3 4 5
ACTIVITY	
MOVEMENT	1 2 3 4 5
PARTICIPATION	1 2 3 4 5
CONVERSATION	1 2 3 4 5

CHAMPs Expectations v. Reality Rating Sheet

CONVERSATION	1 2 3 4 5
HELP (Teacher Attention)	1 2 3 4 5
ACTIVITY	
MOVEMENT	1 2 3 4 5
PARTICIPATION	1 2 3 4 5
CONVERSATION	1 2 3 4 5

CONVERSATION	1 2 3 4 5
HELP (Teacher Attention)	1 2 3 4 5
ACTIVITY	
MOVEMENT	1 2 3 4 5
PARTICIPATION	1 2 3 4 5
CONVERSATION	1 2 3 4 5

CONVERSATION	1 2 3 4 5
HELP (Teacher Attention)	1 2 3 4 5
ACTIVITY	
MOVEMENT	1 2 3 4 5
PARTICIPATION	1 2 3 4 5
CONVERSATION	1 2 3 4 5

CONVERSATION	1 2 3 4 5
HELP (Teacher Attention)	1 2 3 4 5
ACTIVITY	
MOVEMENT	1 2 3 4 5
PARTICIPATION	1 2 3 4 5
CONVERSATION	1 2 3 4 5

CONVERSATION	1 2 3 4 5
HELP (Teacher Attention)	1 2 3 4 5
ACTIVITY	
MOVEMENT	1 2 3 4 5
PARTICIPATION	1 2 3 4 5
CONVERSATION	1 2 3 4 5

CONVERSATION	1 2 3 4 5
HELP (Teacher Attention)	1 2 3 4 5
ACTIVITY	
MOVEMENT	1 2 3 4 5
PARTICIPATION	1 2 3 4 5
CONVERSATION	1 2 3 4 5

Once you have completed the form, review the information. Use it to determine whether you need to reteach the expectations for any of the activities or transitions. You may also wish to share the information with your supervisor and discuss ideas for improving student behavior. The following may be of help as you interpret your information.

> —*If you rated all the activities and transitions with a "4" or a "5," keep doing what you are doing. (If you are not sure what it is you're doing that's making the difference, you might consider videotaping yourself and/or asking your supervisor to observe you and give you feedback. It is important to know what it is you do well so that you can continue to do it!)*

> —*If you rated a couple activities/transitions with a "2" or "3," consider reteaching your expectations for those particular activities/transitions. When you reteach, emphasize the part of the expectation that students had the most trouble with (e.g., Participation).*

> —*If you rated more that half of the activities/transitions with a "1," "2," or "3," discuss the information from this chapter with your supervisor and ask for assistance in managing student behavior.*

NOTE: You may want to involve students in the rating process. If you choose to do this, explain the purpose and procedures to students ahead of time. Be sure to tell students that their feedback should contain NO references to individual students who did not meet expectations.

DISCUSS IT

Arrange with a group of colleagues to read Chapter 5 and do the Take Action activity for this chapter. Then schedule a meeting at which the group can discuss the following topics/questions.

1. Have each person share a behavioral or academic problem involving a student (or students) that has occurred during a small group work period. Remember to use objective reporting, not jargon, labels, or conclusions. After each person has shared, spend five to ten minutes, as a group, on each problem-brainstorming ideas that might help the student(s). If the group can't think of ideas, skim through Chapter 5 to see if any ideas from the chapter could be applicable. (REMINDER: Any changes in procedures should be cleared with a supervisor first.)

2. Have each person share any useful ideas that were gained from working through the Take Action activity for this chapter.

CHAPTER 6

Supervising Independent Work Periods

As a paraeducator, your job at some point is likely to involve supporting classroom instruction. Supporting instruction can assume a variety of forms in addition to working with a small group (see Chapter 5). For example, you may be asked to circulate among and monitor the students while your supervising teacher delivers instruction to the entire class. In this case your responsibilities may include things like keeping students focused on the lesson with gentle verbal and nonverbal reminders to pay attention to the teacher, or monitoring student participation and signaling the teacher that students have completed one step of a project and are ready for the next direction. Or you might be asked to support instruction by participating in a role play with the teacher or even by presenting part of a lesson. One of the most common ways paraeducators support instruction is by supervising a small or large group of students who are working independently on paper/pencil tasks. This generally occurs when the supervising teacher is doing something else and the students working independently do not yet have the maturity to stay focused on their work without adult supervision.

This chapter provides suggestions and strategies to help you effectively support instruction when supervising independent work periods. Keep in mind that the information is applicable to any of the situations described in the first paragraph.

The specific tasks in Chapter 6 are:

1. Be clear about the expectations for students and the expectations for you.

2. Manage independent work periods effectively.

NOTE: Supporting instruction can also involve helping an individual student while the teacher delivers instruction to the entire class. Chapter 7 (Working with an Individual Student) covers information for a paraeducator who works with the same student all day. The suggestions and strategies in that chapter are applicable for someone who works with an individual student for only one or two instructional periods as well.

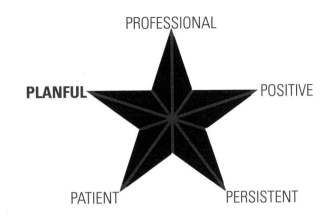

PROFESSIONAL

PLANFUL

POSITIVE

PATIENT

PERSISTENT

TASK 1:

Be clear about the expectations for students and the expectations for you.

*T*o effectively supervise a small or large group of students working independently, you need to find out from your supervising teacher(s) what is expected of the students and of you. If you don't know what the teacher wants, you will not know whether or how you are supposed to help students with their work, for example. You will not know if students are allowed to work together during the time period or if they are supposed to do the work entirely on their own. Being clear about the expectations for this type of job assignment is part of being planful, which is a critical trait for a successful paraeducator.

Try to discuss the expectations with your immediate supervisor prior to actually supervising any independent work period. At the end of this task, you will find two reproducible worksheets—one that addresses the expectations for students during independent work and one that addresses the expectations for you. If you super-

vise more than one independent work period (for the same supervisor or for different supervisors), get information for each different assignment. Different teachers are likely to have different expectations for independent work, and one teacher may have different expectations for different types of independent work periods. For example, say you are supervising in a fifth grade teacher's room in the morning during math and in the afternoon during social studies. The teacher may allow students to work together during the social studies independent work time, but not allow the students to talk when they are doing their independent math work.

Finally, there may be times, as you supervise independent student work, when you feel that a particular work period would go more smoothly if the expectations were different. If you choose to present your thoughts to your supervising teacher, be sure that you do so in a constructive rather than a critical manner. Also, be prepared to accept it if the teacher chooses not to follow through on your suggestions.

HOW TO DO IT:

- **For each independent work period you supervise, find out from the supervising teacher what the expectations are for students.**

Knowing the supervising teacher's expectations for students is critical because you need to know, in detail, which student behaviors are to be encouraged and which behaviors are to be corrected. Following this "How To Do It" section is a reproducible two-page worksheet (Figure 6.1) entitled CHAMPs Expectations for Students During Independent Work. Make a copy of this worksheet for each independent work period you supervise and use it to guide your discussion with the supervising teacher for that period. The CHAMPs acronym is used to prompt you to find out the details of the expectations for students in the areas of Conversation, Help,

is expected of them, so it may be sufficient to periodically remind them how to meet the expectations. On the other hand, if it is the beginning of the school year or you are working with a new group of students who have not been in the setting before, someone needs to teach the students what the expectations are for responsible behavior during this independent work period. NOTE: In Chapter 5, Task 3, you will find suggestions for teaching expectations that you may wish to review and discuss with your supervising teacher.

- **For each independent work period you supervise, find out from the supervising teacher exactly how you are expected to monitor the students.**

You need to ask your supervising teacher whether you are supposed to circulate among students and/or visually scan the setting as they

PARA-PROS WILL	WHEREAS, PARA-CONS TEND TO:
• Ask questions of the teacher until they know EXACTLY how students are expected to behave during independent work.	• Be too shy to find out what the teacher expects of students during independent work. • Not ask questions because they are so arrogant they feel they know better than the teacher how the students should behave during independent work.

Activity, Movement and Participation. You need to know whether or not you are expected to teach the students the behavioral expectations for the independent work period. If you are, ask your supervising teacher exactly how he or she would like you to do this. If the teacher has taught the students the expectations, find out whether and how you should review them with students. For example, if you are assigned to work in a classroom in the middle of the school year, the students probably already know what

are working. Although we recommend doing both, what you should and can do will be dictated by your supervising teacher's expectations and any other job responsibilities you are expected to carry out during the time period. In addition, you may wish to ask the teacher whether there are certain areas of the classroom or certain students that you should pay particular attention to as you monitor. This might include students who are quiet and shy as well as those who tend to have trouble behaving responsibly.

LET ME TRY AND REPEAT BACK YOU EXPECTATIONS, SO YOU CAN LET ME KNOW IF I FULLY UNDERSTAND WHAT YOU WANT ME TO DO.

whether or not students can get help from the teacher, if he or she is in the room.

- **For each independent work period you supervise, find out from the supervising teacher what reinforcement procedures you should use to encourage responsible student behavior.**

Any time you are working with students, you should be prepared to give them positive feedback when they are behaving responsibly. When supervising independent work periods, you need to ask your supervising teacher whether or not there is some kind of structured reinforcement point system in place—either for the entire group or for individual students. If there is, be sure to ask the teacher whether you are to award points throughout the independent work period or only at the end. In addition to reinforcing responsible behavior, check with your supervisor about whether and how you might reinforce the students' academic performance.

- **For each independent work period you supervise, find out from the supervising teacher how you are to respond to various kinds of student misbehavior.**

Once you know from the teacher how students are expected to behave, you then need to know how you are supposed to correct misbehavior. Specifically, you need to know whether there are established corrective consequences for certain misbehaviors and whether there are any correction procedures that you should avoid. In addition, you may wish to ask the teacher about procedures for getting students to quiet down if the noise level is getting too high or be completely silent if you need to make an announcement.

- **For each independent work period you supervise, find out from the supervising teacher what your responsibilities are in terms of providing help and academic assistance to students.**

You need to find out from your supervisor what procedures students are supposed to use to signal that they need your help. If the teacher does not already have procedures in place, you may wish to suggest something like giving each student a "Help" flag or card that they can put at the corner of their desk when they need a question answered. You can teach students that they should continue working once they have put up the flag and that you will come over to them as soon as you can.

You also need to find out from your supervisor exactly what kind of academic assistance you are expected to provide students. That is, should you merely direct the student to the page with the correct answer or should you walk the student through the steps to getting the correct answer? Another question to consider is

- **For each independent work period you supervise, find out from the supervising teacher whether and how you are expected to provide him or her with information about the students' behavior and academic performance.**

The last bit of information you need from your supervising teacher has to do with any feedback the teacher would like from you on how the students behaved and on how they did on the assigned work. In particular, you should ask the teacher exactly what kind of information he or she wants regarding behavior and academic performance (e.g., whether any, some, or all of the students had trouble), how often he or she wants the information (e.g., daily, weekly, or just when there is a problem), and how you are to provide the information (e.g., on a written form, in a face-to-face meeting).

- **Once you know the expectations for students and for you, follow through consistently—that is, arrive on time and cheerfully carry out your duties each day.**

Para-Pros carry out the teacher's expectations, whether or not they agree with them and whether or not the teacher is in the room. Para-Cons tend to let students behave in ways that are different than the teacher's expectations if the teacher is not in the room.

Figure 6.1: Reproducible Form

CHAMP Expectations for Students During Independent Work

Group: _____

Supervisor: _____ Schedule: _____

CONVERSATION

Can students engage in conversations with each other while doing their work?

If yes, can they compare answers?

With whom can they speak (how far away)?

How many students can be involved in a single conversation?

How long can a conversation last?

HELP

How do students get questions answered? How do students get your attention?

If students have to wait for help, what should they do while they wait?

ACTIVITY

What is the type of activity (answering study questions, boardwork, writing in journals)?
(NOTE: This may vary from day to day.)

Figure 6.1 Continued

MOVEMENT

Can students get out of their seats during the activity?

If yes, acceptable reasons include:

Pencil	Hand in/pick up materials
Drink	Restroom
Other:	

Do they need permission?

PARTICIPATION

What behaviors show that students are participating fully and responsibly?

What behaviors show that a student is not participating?

Figure 6. 2: Reproducible Form

Independent Work Supervision: Procedures and Expectations

Supervisor: _____ Schedule: _____

What responsibilities, if any, do I have in addition to supervising the students who are working independently?

What are my responsibilities in terms of communicating (i.e., teaching and/or reviewing) the behavioral expectations to students? Exactly how am I to teach and/or review the expectations?

Exactly how am I expected to monitor the students while they are working independently?

Exactly how am I expected to provide help and/or academic assistance to students while they are working independently?

Exactly what reinforcement procedures should I use to encourage responsible student behavior?

What correction procedures should I use to respond to student misbehavior? Are there procedures I should avoid? Are there specific corrective consequences for specific misbehaviors?

Exactly how should I give you (the teacher) information on the students' behavior during the independent work times?

Exactly how should I give you (the teacher) information on the students' academic performance during the independent work times?

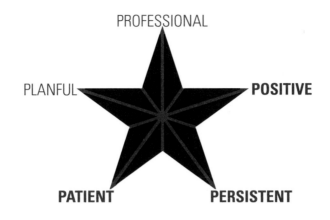

PROFESSIONAL

PLANFUL

POSITIVE

PATIENT

PERSISTENT

TASK 2:

Manage independent work periods effectively.

In this task, we provide specific information and tips on how to effectively support instruction when supervising independent work periods. Please note that the strategies and suggestions included can be applied to a variety of situations in which you might be asked to support instruction (e.g., you are responsible for monitoring and assisting students while the teacher presents a whole class lesson). In addition to monitoring student behavior, reinforcing responsible student behavior, and correcting irresponsible student behavior, when you support instruction you also need to be prepared to provide help and academic assistance to those students who need it.

We have highlighted the "Positive", "Patient", and "Persistent" points of the star because all of these qualities are required as you support instruction. That is, you need to set a positive tone that communicates you are there to assist the students with their work in addition to encouraging their responsible behavior and correcting any misbehavior.

As you consider the information presented in this task, remember that you need to do things the way your supervisor expects you to do them. If you choose to share any of the suggestions or strategies presented in this task with your supervisor, do so in a thoughtful and constructive manner.

HOW TO DO IT:

- **Communicate the expectations to students (as needed).**

Your supervising teacher may want you to teach or review the behavioral expectations for the independent work period to students. Your supervising teacher should tell you how he or she would like you to do this, but you may also wish to review Chapter 5, Task 3 for additional information and suggestions.

- **Circulate among the students as much as possible.**

Unless you are assigned by your immediate supervisor to do something in addition to supervising the independent work (e.g., grading papers or working with a small group of students), move among the students throughout the entire independent work period. It is important to move slowly because you do not want to distract students from their work. Be unpredictable in the route you take as you circulate—you don't want to let students in one part of the room know that it will be several minutes before you will get over to them. Be intentional as you circulate. That is, if you have found that certain students have a tendency to misbehave, spend a greater percentage of your time circulating near those students. Your presence will help prompt the students to meet expectations.

If you are expected to do other tasks in addition to supervising students working independently, try to circulate among the students as frequently as possible. For example, if you are grading papers, you might get up and circulate throughout the room every five minutes or so. If you are working with a small group, it may not be possible to circulate among the students working at their seats. In that case, the following information on visual scanning is particularly important.

WHEN YOU SUPERVISE, YOU CAN COMMUNICATE POSITIVE OR NEGATIVE EXPECTATIONS.

• Visually scan the students working independently.

As you circulate, also make a point of sweeping your eyes to all parts of the room where students are working independently. Think of scanning as collecting a quick picture of each student to determine whether the student needs help, is on-task, or is engaged in some kind of misbehavior. Use the information you get to help you decide what to do next. For example, if you notice one student signaling for help and three others at the back of the room looking sheepish and trying not to giggle, you might decide to acknowledge the student who needs help, but go immediately to the three students who, if left alone, seem likely to get into trouble. "Talia, thank you for raising your hand; I will be there in just a moment."

You can continue to scan even while interacting with a student or a small group. For example, if you have stopped to help a student with a math problem, you can look up periodically or even stand up if necessary, to get your "picture" of what is going on in the rest of the room. Then you can decide whether to continue helping the student or attend to something more urgent that needs your attention.

Scanning is especially important if you cannot circulate. For example, if you have to grade papers or do some other task that confines you to a particular space, make a point of looking up to scan frequently. That way students will know that even though you are not physically near them, you are aware of what they are doing.

As you scan, remember that you are looking for positive behaviors as well as problems. Use every opportunity to reinforce responsible behavior. For example, if you notice that a student who is often off-task is working diligently, you can go over and acknowledge the student.

• Provide assistance to students who signal or appear to need help.

When a student signals that he or she needs assistance, acknowledge the signal as soon as you can. If possible, go to the student and ask,

"May I help you?" If you are busy doing something else (e.g., helping another student), let the student know you will be there in a moment.

When you help a student, use a quiet voice so that you do not disturb other students. This also lets you model for everyone that quiet behavior is expected. When you can, get to the student's level by pulling up a chair, going down on one knee, or bending over to look at the student's work. You don't want to invade a student's space, but it's generally less intimidating for students to have someone close to or on the same level as they are rather than standing over them.

Help students by guiding them to the correct answer. For example, if a student is having trouble with a math problem involving multiple steps, ask the student questions such as, "What do you do first in this type of problem? What do you do next?" If there's a step the student does not know how to do, or has been doing wrong, tell the student the correct way to do that step, and continue to guide the student until he or she gets the answer. Avoid simply telling students the answers to specific items because that will not help them learn how to complete their work independently.

Be encouraging. As a student completes steps or answers questions independently, say things like, "You definitely know how to do that" and "Yes, that is correct." If a student struggles or does not know how to do a particular step, say things like, "This can be tricky, let me show you" or "When you do this kind of problem, if you _____, you'll be able to get the correct answer." Avoid statements like, "Oh, you know how to do this kind of problem" or "I showed you how to do this yesterday." If a student doesn't remember what to do, these kinds of comments provide no assistance and are likely to make the student feel stupid.

If a particular student seems to need an excessive amount of assistance over several days, share that information with your immediate supervisor. Tell the supervisor the types of questions or difficulties the student is having and ask whether you should be responding differently.

The student may just be struggling with a new skill or concept, and will no longer have so many questions once she gets it. However, it's also possible that the student is "over her head" and could benefit from additional instruction, modified assignments, or being in a different instructional group. Sometimes students ask for help even though they don't really need it, because it's a way to get adult attention. Identifying why a student needs so much help and what to do about it is the responsibility of your supervisor. Your responsibility is to let the supervisor know what is happening and to carry out any suggestions your supervisor makes.

- ## Reinforce responsible student behavior.

When students are meeting the expectations for responsible behavior, you want to provide positive feedback. To do this in a manner that is not distracting to students who are working independently, go to students individually and quietly tell them what they are doing well. If directed to do so by your supervisor, provide feedback on the quality of student work as well.

169

Thus, when giving positive feedback you might say things like:

—*You are almost finished and we still have 15 minutes left, Maria.*

—*Tina, you are aligning the columns of these problems very neatly. That is important when doing multi-column addition.*

—*Jacob, you are using your time very wisely.*

—*Marco, this is the neatest handwriting I have seen you use.*

—*Allison, you are staying so focused you are getting a lot completed.*

—*Tyronne, you are showing a great deal of responsibility during this worktime.*

If you find that this sort of verbal praise seems distracting to students, you might experiment with non-verbal feedback. For example, as you walk by the desk of a student who is working hard, you might give a "thumbs up" signal to let him know that you notice his positive behavior. Or, if a student looks up briefly from her work and makes eye contact with you, you might smile and nod your head to communicate that you have seen her working and are pleased.

If the supervising teacher uses a point or token system, find out whether you are supposed to award the points/tokens throughout the work period (as you circulate) or only at the end. Be careful not to "play favorites." Points should be awarded objectively, based on the actual behavior of the students on that day. Do not let yourself hold any sort of grudge based on misbehavior from previous days.

• Respond effectively to student misbehavior.

When supervising independent seatwork, implement the basics for correcting misbehavior that were introduced in Chapter 3, Task 5. That

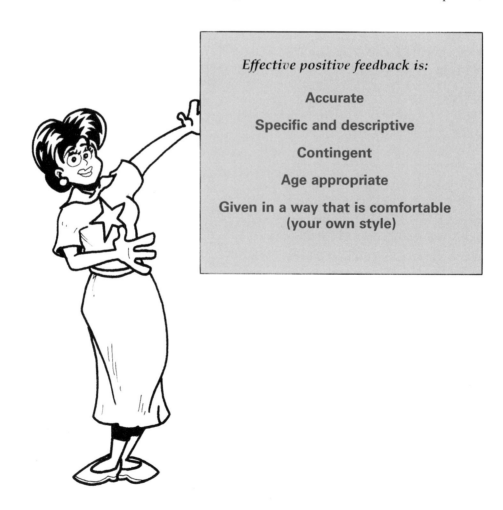

Effective positive feedback is:

Accurate

Specific and descriptive

Contingent

Age appropriate

Given in a way that is comfortable (your own style)

is, you need to be professional, patient and calm, persistent and consistent, and planful. As you apply those basic concepts to correcting misbehavior during independent work periods, you might also want to keep the following specific tips in mind.

—*Do not correct misbehavior from across the room—go to the student who is misbehaving.*

—*Correct quietly so as not to disturb other students and to avoid having the interaction between you and the misbehaving student become a public display.*

—*Intervene as soon as you observe the misbehavior. Do not let a misbehavior go on because it will usually get worse and be harder to correct later.*

—*Do not engage in arguing with a student or students. State the misbehavior and, when applicable, the corrective consequence. If a student starts to argue with you, simply reiterate the misbehavior and the corrective consequence. Be sure to discuss any ongoing compliance problems with your supervisor.*

Following is a list of corrective consequences that are appropriate and effective for misbehavior that occurs during independent seatwork periods. They are included here for information purposes only, although you may wish to discuss them with your supervisor. In practice, you need to implement the corrective consequences your supervisor has instructed you to use.

—*Verbal reprimand*

A verbal reprimand consists of going to the student or students engaged in a misbehavior (e.g., talking when they should be working quietly) and stating the positive expectation. "Now is a time for working quietly with no talking."

—*Time-out*

This requires that a time-out area, which can be as simple as a chair in a low traffic area of the classroom, already be set up. The maximum length of time a student should be assigned for time-out is three minutes for primary students (grades K-3) and five minutes for older students. When in time-out, a student should not be allowed to do anything, and should be held accountable for completing the assignment the class is working on.

—*Demerits*

Demerits are essentially negative points which, when accumulated, lead to a bigger consequence. For example, there may be a policy in a middle school resource room that each time you have to remind a student to get back to work, that student receives one demerit. If the student gets more than three demerits in one class period, he or she would be assigned an after-school detention.

—*Point fines*

Point fines, which require that a positive reinforcement system be in place, involve having a student lose one point for each infraction.

—*Time-owed*

Time-owed involves taking away a small amount of time (e.g., one minute) from an activity such as recess for each infraction. Never use time-owed unless instructed to do so by your supervisor, because students who owe time require supervision. If approved by your supervisor, you might have middle or high school students owe 15 seconds off the next passing period for each infraction. If a student exhibited four misbehaviors, she would be kept one minute after class.

—*Change in seat*

If two or more students have trouble staying on-task when they sit together, they should not be allowed to sit together. If one student bothers other students, that student's desk should be moved to a point in the room that is away from others. Once a student who has had his seat changed demonstrates responsible behavior for a few days, you can try moving the student back to the original seating arrangement.

CHAPTER 6  ACTIVITIES

THINK ABOUT IT

Use the following chart to evaluate your familiarity with the material presented in this chapter. When you have completed this activity, enter reminders about the tasks you wanted to reread or discuss into your planning calendar.

Figure 6.3 Reproducible Form

	The information was not applicable to my situation.	The information was familiar. I consistently implement the strategies presented.	The information was useful. I should reread this task at least once more this year.	Some of the information was new. I should reread this task within a month.	Much of the information was new. I should discuss it with my supervisor or with other paraeducators.
TASK 1: Be clear about the expectations for students and the expectations for you.	0	1	2	3	4
TASK 2: Manage independent work periods effectively.	0	1	2	3	4

(NOTE: On pages 205-210, in the back of the book, you will find a complete chart of all the tasks in the book. You may wish to summarize the information from each individual chapter on this single chart.)

TAKE ACTION

For one day, monitor the degree to which student behavior during an independent work period you supervise matches the CHAMPs expectations for that period (see Task 1). That is, as you supervise, consider how well the students are meeting the expectations for Conversation, Help, Movement, and Participation during that period. The one-page form in Figure 6.4 allows you to rate student behavior during independent work on the following scale:

5 = All students met expectations

4 = All but one or two students met expectations

3 = Most students met expectations

2 = About half the class met expectations

1 = Most students did not meet expectations

At the end of the period, review the information. If you find that for each of the four areas (Conversation, Help, Movement, and Participating) you are able to give a rating of 5, congratulate the students on their maturity and responsibility. If you rate any of the areas with a 4, reteach those specific expectations to the few students who had problems. For any 3 rating, reteach the expectations to the entire group for a few days. And if you have any 1 or 2 ratings, arrange to discuss the situation with your supervisor. You may want to consider asking for assistance in setting up a plan for improving student behavior.

NOTE: Figure 6.4 can be reproduced on a transparency if you want to involve the students in discussing the ratings.

CHAMPs Expectations v. Reality Rating Scale

Independent Work Period: _____

5 = All students met expectations

4 = All but one or two students met expectations

3 = Most students met expectations

2 = About half the class met expectations

1 = Most students did not meet expectations

CONVERSATION	1 2 3 4 5
HELP (Teacher Attention)	1 2 3 4 5
ACTIVITY: Independent Seatwork	
MOVEMENT	1 2 3 4 5
PARTICIPATION	1 2 3 4 5

DISCUSS IT

Arrange with a group of colleagues to read Chapter 6 and do the Take Action activity for this chapter. Then schedule a meeting at which the group can discuss the following topics/questions.

1. Have each person share a behavioral or academic problem involving a student (or students) that has occurred during an independent work period. Remember to use objective reporting, not jargon, labels, or conclusions. After each person has shared, spend five to ten minutes, as a group, on each problem-brainstorming ideas that might help the student(s). If the group can't think of ideas, skim through Chapter 6 to see if any ideas from the chapter could be applicable. *(REMINDER: Any changes in procedures should be cleared with a supervisor first.)*

2. Have each person share any useful ideas that were gained from working through the **Take Action** activity for this chapter.

CHAPTER 7

Working With an Individual Student

When a school or district determines that an individual student cannot function successfully on his or her own, an adult may be assigned to that student. One-on-one assistance is often necessary when a student has "high needs"—that is, severe physical disabilities that necessitate medical and/or mobility assistance or severe mental or emotional disabilities that result in behavior problems that interfere with the student's ability to learn and/or with the learning and safety of other students. At some point as a paraeducator, you may be assigned to work virtually all day with a single individual student.

Working with a "high-needs" student can be a very difficult, but also very rewarding, job assignment. It can be difficult because whenever you work with a student who has fairly involved disabilities, you have to keep a balanced perspective. You must be patient and compassionate of the student's disabilities, yet not fall into pitying or feeling sorry for the student. You must have high expectations for the student, while making sure the expectations are realistic given the student's disabilities. You must learn to give the student as much help as necessary, but as little help as possible. And very likely, you will have to do all of this while working with a team of other adults, all of whom have some say in the student's educational experiences. This team may involve several different teachers, the principal, the special education director, a physical therapist, the student's parents, and so on.

At the same time, working closely with an individual student has the potential to be incredibly satisfying. Quite literally, you can make a big difference in a student's life because often it is your assistance that makes it possible for the student to even be in school. Furthermore, you have the opportunity to develop a close relationship with the student and possibly with the student's family.

There are some important reminders and cautions to keep in mind when you work with an individual student. Confidentiality is critical! You will be working closely with the student and possibly the family, and you must be very careful not to gossip, make judgments, or talk about things that are private family business. At the same time, because you are working so closely with the student, you may be the first to notice evidence of a problem (e.g., abuse). In the unlikely event that this sort of concern should arise, talk to your primary supervisor immediately.

Finally, remember to be flexible. Although you may be assigned to work with the one student, you are likely to be asked to do other things (e.g., playground duty) as well. You should carry out any other duties cheerfully and to the best of your abilities.

The specific tasks in Chapter 7 are:

1. **Understand your role as part of the team that will help the student become as independent as possible.**

2. **Get relevant background information about the student.**

3. **Be clear about what is expected of the student and what is expected of you in all situations.**

4. **Interact productively with the student.**

5. **Interact appropriately with the student's family.**

NOTE: Although this chapter is geared for a paraeducator who works with one student all day, the information and suggestions are also applicable to a situation in which a paraeducator works with an individual student for only one or two periods during the day.

PROFESSIONAL

PLANFUL

POSITIVE

PATIENT

PERSISTENT

TASK 1:

Understand your role as part of the team that will help the student become as independent as possible.

*P*art of what can make working with one student so difficult is the number of adults who may be involved in planning for that student. That is, you may have to deal with multiple teachers in both general and special education, administrative staff including the building principal and special education director or supervisor, the student's family, specialists such as physical therapists (PT), occupational therapists (OT), speech/language clinicians, counselors, psychologists, and possibly even a family advocate or one or more attorneys. All of these adults are likely to have more input and more authority in designing the student's Individualized Education Program (IEP) than you. Yet, you are likely to be the school-based person with the most direct contact with the student, and possibly the one who carries the greatest day-to-day responsibility for following through on that program.

In some ways, it's like a funnel. Everyone provides input that results in a program for the student—which you then have to implement. (see Figure 7.1)

This task provides suggestions on how you can successfully fulfill your role as part of the team who implements the student's IEP, and not get caught in the middle of different adults with different ideas about carrying out the plan. The more team members involved, the more important and difficult this becomes.

HOW TO DO IT:

- **Be clear about who you go to for instructions and information regarding this assignment (i.e., your primary supervisor).**

When you work as a one-on-one assistant with an individual student, you are likely to be given information and instructions about the student from the following individuals: a) your primary supervisor; b) the person who is officially responsible for ensuring that the student's

Figure 7.1

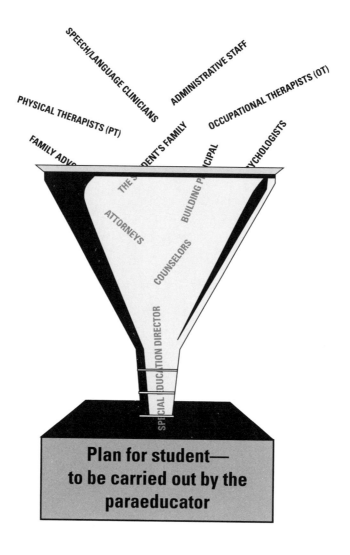

Individualized Education Program is carried out (i.e., the student's case manager); c) teachers into whose rooms you go with the student for classwork; and d) specialists such as the physical therapist or school psychologist who also work with the student. While all the information and instructions may be important, it is imperative that you know who has responsibility for ensuring that YOU carry out your job assignment and to whom you can go with any questions or concerns you may have.

If you are unclear about who your primary supervisor for this assignment is, be professionally and politely assertive about getting clarification. Often, your primary supervisor will be the student's case manager, so that can be a good place to start. Explain that to avoid any problems later, you need to know who you ask if you have questions about how to carry out the student's program or whether or not to do something you have been told to do by the student's parents or another staff member. If your primary supervisor turns out to be someone other than the student's case manager, you need to know what your relationship should be to the case manager and any teachers the student has. Specifically, you need to know who will give you information on what is expected of the student and what is expected of you in various situations and settings.

Consider the following scenarios. In each case, you should know who in authority you would go to for input and a decision. If you are unable to get clarification on who your primary supervisor is from anyone else, ask the building principal.

> —The student complains that he cannot do the work he is being assigned in a regular classroom, and you agree that the work is not within the student's ability level.

> —A general education teacher tells you that you should help other students in the room and if the student you are assigned to has to wait a few minutes when she needs help, you should make her wait.

> —The student seems to do fine in most situations, but there is one class in which the teacher seems particularly hostile toward the student and the student is beginning to rebel.

• **Find out from your primary supervisor what your responsibilities are in terms of attending IEP meetings, parent conferences, and any other types of meetings.**

If you are expected to attend these types of meetings, and they occur during school hours, find out from your supervisor how your duties with the student will be covered when you are at a meeting. If the meetings occur outside your scheduled work hours, you may need to ask about additional payment or some form of compensation time.

When you do participate in meetings about the student, listen more than you talk. If someone suggests something that you don't understand, let the person finish speaking and ask for

clarification using an "I" statement or question. "I am a bit unclear about what I should do. How do you suggest I handle it if . . . ." If you disagree with what has been presented or suggested, express yourself in a thoughtful and respectful manner—without arguing or pressing your point. As much as possible, explain your concern in terms of the needs of the student. Remember, once you have voiced your opinion, all final decisions about what you will actually do rest with your supervisor.

- **Find out from your primary supervisor what your responsibilities are in terms of communicating with the student's family.**

As the school-based person who potentially has the most contact with the student, communication between the school and home may end up going through you. You need to be very clear about what/how you are expected to communicate with the student's family. See Task 5 of this chapter for more information on this topic.

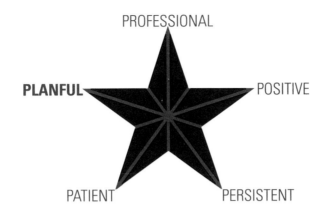

PROFESSIONAL

PLANFUL — POSITIVE

PATIENT   PERSISTENT

TASK 2:

Get relevant background information about the student.

*I*n order to work effectively with an individual student, you will want to find out as much relevant background information about the student as possible. The "Planful" point of the star is highlighted because this information will allow you to be more prepared and thoughtful when assisting the student. That is, having important background information will help you help the student function more independently and successfully in each school setting.

The "How To Do It" section of this task walks you through some of the issues you will want to discuss with your supervisor to ensure that you have all the necessary information.

HOW TO DO IT:

- **Find out about the goals, objectives, plans, and any record keeping systems that have already been established for the student.**

Whether or not your immediate supervisor chooses to share the student's complete IEP with you, you should know what the student's predominate disability is and what the major academic and behavioral goals and objectives are for the student.

Also find out if you are supposed to keep records of any kind on the student's behavior/performance. For example, you may be asked to count and record the number of times a certain behavior occurs, or to note when assignments are completed, or to maintain an anecdotal log of what the student does throughout each day. If the members of the student's team want you to collect any information, it is because that information will help them determine the effectiveness of the student's program. Therefore, be sure you are very clear about exactly what information you are expected to collect and how, so that you can follow through. Find out how often and in what form you are supposed to share the information you collect (e.g., summarized on a chart, transcribed onto a special form, entered into a computer, etc.). Finally, in addition to any regular sharing of information, you might want to ask about any special circumstances or events that you should report to your supervisor.

• **Find out whether there are any particularly difficult behavioral/social issues you should be aware of.**

Ask your supervisor whether the student has a past history of behavioral difficulties (e.g., physical violence). If behavior problems are the reason the student has been assigned a one-on-one adult, ask for detailed answers to the following questions:

—*What kind of problem behaviors might the student exhibit?*

—*What are you expected to do if the student exhibits dangerous behavior? Whom/how do you call for assistance?*

You need to know whether/how you are expected to intervene in dangerous situations—for example, whether you are expected to restrain the student. Please note that we recommend you never restrain a student unless you have been given training and written directions on exactly what to do.

—*Are there particular events, people, subjects, and/or activities that seem to "set the student off?"*

Ask your supervisor whether the student has any known "triggers," and what you can/should do to help the student in the presence of these trigger events.

A student with a history of behavioral/emotional problems is likely to have a Behavior Improvement Plan (BIP) that should outline in detail the kinds of things that can/should be done to help the student succeed behaviorally. If the student does not have a BIP, or if your supervisor chooses not to share the written BIP with you, ask lots of "What should I do if . . . ." kinds questions. In particular, be sure you understand when and how to implement any token economies or other reward systems for reinforcing responsible behavior and exactly how you are to respond to misbehavior.

• **Find out about any medical issues you should be aware of.**

Another very important area about which you need information concerns any medications the student may be taking. For example, you need to know if you have any responsibility in terms of storing and/or administering medication for the student. If you do, ask questions until you know EXACTLY what you are supposed to do, at what times, and how. (If possible, get this in writing.) Even if you have no responsibility for storing and/or administering the medication, you still should know the times and locations the student will receive medication at school so you can make sure the student gets to the appointed place(s) at the right time(s).

Furthermore, you should find out whether there are side effects to any medication the student takes, at home or at school. Ask what you should watch for and what you should do (i.e., to whom you should report it) if you observe the side effects. Keep in mind that some side effects can be immediately life threatening, others more cumulatively damaging. In either case, you should be aware of any potential side effects that might constitute an emergency or a danger to the student.

If you are given written information about what you are to do and when you are to do it regarding medications, follow that information to the letter. If you are not given a written summary, we recommend that you take the time yourself to write out any verbal information/instructions you have been given and that you ask your primary supervisor to review it for accuracy.

• **Find out about any toileting responsibilities.**

When a student has severe physical or cognitive (mental) disabilities, assisting the student with toileting may be part of your job responsibilities. As with medication issues, this is a topic about which you should ask lots of questions to ensure that you understand precisely how to carry out your responsibilities. If you have never had toileting responsibilities for an individual with disabilities, ask your supervisor to demonstrate (or to arrange for someone experienced to demonstrate) exactly what you should do. Then ask that someone observe you carrying out the procedures a couple of times to provide feedback and suggestions before you continue on your own. Be sure you know how you are to meet the student's needs, give the student as much privacy as possible, and protect yourself from any potential accusations of impropriety. For example, you may wish to ask whether another adult will be present when you assist with toileting.

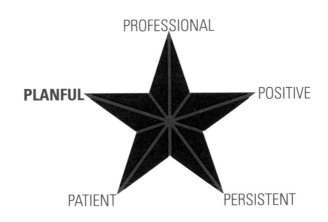

PROFESSIONAL

PLANFUL — POSITIVE

PATIENT — PERSISTENT

TASK 3:

Be clear about what is expected of the student and what is expected of you in all situations.

As first mentioned in Chapter 3, among the most important foundations for effectively managing student behavior are knowing exactly what behaviors are expected of the student and knowing exactly what is expected of you. This can be especially difficult when you work with a single student all day every day because you not only need detailed expectations for each different setting the student goes to, but also for each major type of activity that occurs within each of those settings, and for the transitions between activities/settings.

There is no " How To Do It" section for this task. Instead, we recommend that you start by listing the student's daily schedule, and then complete a copy of the CHAMPs Expectations for an Individual Student worksheet (reproducible Figure 7.3 at the end of this task), for each setting, major activity, and transition in the student's schedule. Consider the following sample schedule (Figure 7.2).

This schedule would require getting detailed expectations information for each of the four class periods taught by the Special Education teacher, the class period taught by the PE

Figure 7.2

SAMPLE STUDENT SCHEDULE	
8:00	Arrival of bus to front of school
8:10	1st period through 3rd period in Special Education classroom
11:15	4th period lunch with general population in cafeteria
12:10	5th period (general ed PE class)
2:00	7th period Special Education classroom
2:50	Dismissal
3:00	Bus departs

teacher, and the class period taught by the History teacher. Specifically, you would need to know the expectations for the major activities that occur within each of those class periods. For example, in the History class you might need to complete one CHAMPs worksheet for lecture or teacher directed activities, one for cooperative group activities, and one for independent work time. Finally, you would need to find out the expectations for the following transitions: a) bus to Special Ed room; b) Special Ed room to the cafeteria; c) lunch recess to 5th period; d) passing periods between 5th, 6th, and 7th periods; and 4) Special Ed room to bus at the end of the day. In addition to knowing what is expected of the student in all of those situations (so that you will know which behaviors to reinforce and which to correct), you would need to know exactly how you are expected to reinforce, correct, and assist the student.

Once again the Planful point of the star is highlighted because it is advance information and planning that will help you do your job effectively. Without planning, it would be very difficult to ensure that you are meeting the needs of the student and carrying out the expectations of the (potentially many) different adults who have some say in developing and implementing the student's program.

Figure 7.3: Reproducible Form

CHAMPs Expectations for an Individual Student

Setting: _____

Supervisor: _____ Time _____

CONVERSATION

Is the student allowed to converse with other students during this activity?

If so, about what?

For how long?

With how many other students?

HELP

Is the student allowed to talk to me (the assistant)? How should he get my attention?

Is the student allowed to talk to other adults (e.g., classroom teacher)? If so, how does he get their attention?

In class, should I help the student with academic work?

If so, how much?

Should I help other students as well?

If the student is assigned homework, do I monitor performance and completion or not?

Figure 7.3 Continued

ACTIVITY

Will the activity vary from day to day (e.g. a different assignment) or will the lesson expectations stay the same each day?

MOVEMENT

Can the student move from one place to another during this time period?

If so, for what reasons?

Should I escort the student, or should the student be allowed to move independently?

PARTICIPATION

During this activity, what does active participation look like and sound like?

What does non-participation look like and sound like?

If the student is not participating, should I correct the student?

If so, how?

If other students are not participating, should I correct them?

If so, how?

What is my responsibility in communicating these expectations to the student?

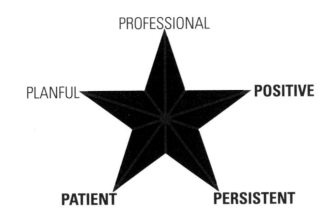

PROFESSIONAL

PLANFUL

POSITIVE

PATIENT

PERSISTENT

TASK 4:

Interact productively with the student.

When you work with one student for the majority of the day, the level of responsibility is awesome. Whether or not the student makes progress will depend not only on how appropriate the plan for the student is, but also on how successfully you help carry out that plan. This task contains tips and techniques for working effectively with an individual student. There are three sections. The first section addresses some "big picture" ideas for helping the student meet academic goals and objectives. Learning can occur despite severe mental or physical disabilities, and in large measure it is your productive interactions with the student that will help him or her achieve his or her academic expectations. The second section reviews strategies for effectively managing student behavior (the kinds of things introduced in Chapter 3) and focuses in particular on how to avoid some of the common difficulties that occur when working with an individual student. The third section provides tips on how to build and maintain a productive relationship with the student—that is, a relationship that encourages the student to trust you and, at the same time, to be as independent from you as his/her disability allows.

The Positive point of the star is highlighted because with the kind of close relationships that often develop in one-on-one situations, the attitude of one person tends to greatly influence the attitude of the other. As you help the student achieve his or her educational goals, your positive attitude and demeanor are essential for giving the student hope and for creating the expectation of ongoing progress. In addition, the student will need lots of positive feedback from you for both academic and behavioral progress. The Patient and Persistent points are highlighted because working with an individual student can be a highly emotional experience—exhilarating and rewarding some of the time, frustrating and aggravating at other times. You need to be patient with errors and setbacks and during times when the student "tests" you, and you need to be persistent in maintaining high, but realistic, expectations about progress.

HOW TO DO IT:

• Help the student succeed with academic goals.

When working with the student, be sure to implement any instructional strategies suggested by your primary supervisor. In fact, it's a good idea to ask your supervisor about strategies that have worked well in the past and those that have not. In addition, you may wish to consider the following broad-based suggestions.

—Remember that success breeds success, and failure breeds frustration and discouragement.

Helping the student succeed is important. The trick is remembering that your ultimate goal is for the student to be able to do the skill independently, creating in him a sense of mastery and success. If you just do the assignment for the student or give him too much assistance, he may actually feel like a failure because he will know that it was you, not he, who did the assignment. On the other hand, when the student is given what you know will be a very difficult assignment, don't let the student try, fail, and end up having to redo the work if that can be avoided. Instead, consider demonstrating for the student how to accurately complete the first third or so of the assignment, working with the student to complete the second part of the assignment together, and then having the student do the last third of the assignment independently. Always try to preteach and practice difficult academic tasks. For example, if you know that the student is facing a challenging test, work directly with the student to prepare. Remember that practice is important. Knowing something on Monday does not mean it will be remembered on Friday. However, if it is practiced and reviewed each day, Monday through Thursday, there is a greater chance it will be remembered on Friday.

—Assist the student with organizational strategies.

If the student struggles with keeping track of materials, writing down assignments, losing completed work, and forgetting to do homework, see if you can help him learn to use age-appropriate strategies for being organized. Ask your primary supervisor for suggestions.

Note: Skills for School Success is an excellent program that teaches organizational strategies, notetaking skills, listening skills and so on.

Skills for School Success

Anita Archer and Mary Gleason (1990)
North Billerica, MA: Curriculum Associates

—Be careful not to (inadvertently) foster the student's dependence on you.

Whether you realize it or not, or intend it or not, having someone become highly dependent on you can be very satisfying. Try not to help the student any more than is necessary. Remember, your job is to help the student be as successful, AND independent, as possible.

• Help the student learn to behave responsibly.

If the student does not know the expectations for a given setting, be sure to communicate those expectations. Use modeling, demonstration, telling the student, and so on to teach and/or review expectations (see Chapter 5, Task 3). Check for understanding by asking the student questions and/or by having the student demonstrate the positive behaviors. Communicate expectations right before each activity for several days, until you are sure the student understands exactly what is expected for each major activity and transition.

Monitor the student's behavior but unless you are immediately needed by the student, avoid hovering. If you are also working with other students, use visual scanning to make sure your student does not need assistance.

Provide positive feedback and follow through on any established reinforcement systems when the student is meeting expectations. If it is not intrusive, give feedback during the activity. Be careful, however, that the feedback does not embarrass or set the student apart from peers. At the end of each activity or transition that has gone well, give the student positive feedback before moving to the next activity or setting.

If the student misbehaves (i.e., behaves in a way that does not meet expectations), correct the student in a calm, consistent manner. This is especially important and can be especially difficult when you work with the same student throughout the day. If the student finds that he can upset you by misbehaving, that is likely to reinforce the misbehavior.

Don't take the student's behavior personally. Sometimes a student will say hurtful things to someone close to drive the person away or to get an emotional reaction. If the student you work with is hurtful, remind yourself that you are an important adult in the student's life and that you cannot let yourself take the student's comments seriously. Do not let yourself hold a grudge or feel resentment toward the student.

When an activity ends and the student has not met all the expectations, plan to provide positive feedback on two things the student did well and help the student set one goal for improvement. This allows you to put positive closure on an activity that was a problem, before transitioning to the next activity.

Watch for any patterns to the student's misbehavior. That is, note whether the student seems to misbehave more around certain people, at particular times, transitions, places, or during subjects. Because you probably have the most contact with the student, you are likely to be in the best position to recognize patterns. Discuss any trends you see with your supervisor. For example, if you notice that the student has trouble with transitions, you might ask your supervisor to help you set up a structured plan for helping the student be more successful during these times.

- **Build a productive relationship with the student.**

Given that you will be working so closely with the student, a productive relationship will be important both for the student's success and so that the two of you can generally enjoy your time together. The first suggestion for building a positive relationship is to listen attentively. Show the student that you are interested in what she says and what she is feeling. Obviously you cannot let this interfere with

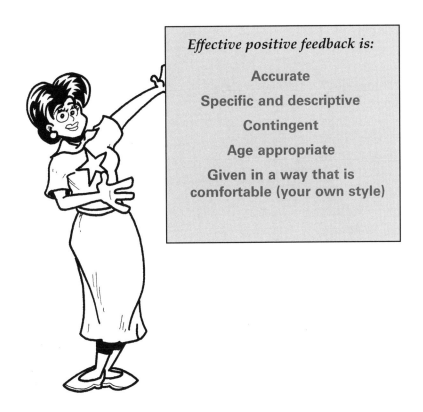

Effective positive feedback is:

Accurate

Specific and descriptive

Contingent

Age appropriate

Given in a way that is comfortable (your own style)

instructional priorities, but throughout the day use all opportunities for less structured interactions.

Also, provide frequent non-contingent acknowledgement of the student. Greet her and periodically ask how she is doing. Talk to her about non-school activities. These kinds of interactions can be especially important after a bad day. That is, saying "Good morning" with a smile demonstrates to the student that the previous bad day is forgotten and that you are

ready for a brand new start. Demonstrate that you are interested in the student as a person, not just that you like her when she behaves well or meets her goals.

Discuss with your supervisor how much to let the student get to know you. Within reason, you may want to give the student a bit of a look into your life outside of school. If you choose to do this, you might occasionally bring in family photos, tell stories about yourself, or talk about your own interests.

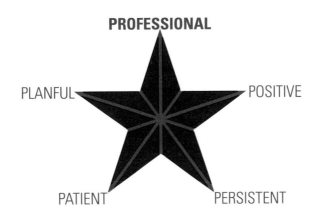

PROFESSIONAL

PLANFUL — POSITIVE

PATIENT — PERSISTENT

TASK 5:

Interact appropriately with the student's family.

NOTE: When we say "the student's family," we mean the student's major caregivers, which can be the student's parent(s), grandparent(s), foster parent(s), etc.

*I*f you are not expected to have direct contact with the student's family, you may choose to simply skim this task. However, if your job responsibilities include communicating with the student's family, the information in this task may help you meet that responsibility more effectively. Note that the Professional point of the star has been highlighted. Remember, the family's perception of the school will be largely influenced by the person with whom they have the most contact—potentially you. Therefore, you need to present yourself in a professional manner at all times. You also need to display professionalism by not allowing personal likes or dislikes to be reflected in your contacts with the student's family.

We suggest that you think of yourself as a communicator or "one who makes known," and that you think of your role when interacting with the family as being a link between home and school. Thus, your job is to make known to the family what is happening at school and to make known to school staff (through your supervisor) any ideas, concerns, questions, or requests that come from the family. It's important not to let any feelings you may have about the student, the student's family, your supervisor, or even the school affect the quality and clarity of the link you create between school and home.

The "How To Do It" section of this chapter begins with a series of questions regarding communicating with the family that you might want to discuss with your supervisor. It then continues with some overall suggestions to keep in mind as you interact with the student's family.

HOW TO DO IT:

• **Find out from your supervisor the details of how you are to communicate with the student's family.**

Your supervisor should give you all the information you need regarding the nature of your interactions with the student's family. The following questions are designed to prompt you as to the kind of information you will need.

—What is the name of the family member(s) with whom you will communicate?

When you initially contact the person, use Mr. or Ms. and the surname, rather than a first name. Ask the person how he or she would prefer to be addressed in the future.

—What is the person's relationship to the student?

—Are there any custody issues/problems you should be aware of? (e.g., Are there particular people you should not share information with? particular people the student should not leave school with?)

—Are there any language or cultural issues to keep in mind when interacting with the family?

—How should you initially contact the family (e.g., to introduce yourself)?

—What form of regular communication should be used? How often should regular communication occur?

Following are possibilities for regular home/school communication that you may wish to review with your supervisor.

—Home/School Daily Communication form

(See Figure 7.4, page 199 at the end of this task.)

If you use this method, make sure it has been explained to the family and that the family understands that the purpose is to create daily two-way communication between home and school.

—Progress charts

If you use progress charts to share daily tracking of particular social or academic behaviors with the family, be sure the family knows how to interpret any information presented.

—Phone calls

—Face to Face contact

—Home visits or school conferences

These are most likely the job of your supervisor.

—Is a Contact Log required? recommended?

(See Figure 7.5, page 200 at the end of this task)

—What is your responsibility for seeing that the family gets school notices, newsletters, and other school communication?

Unfortunately, students with disabilities and their families often do not hear about the science fair or ice cream social or other school functions.

—Are there particular procedures/issues regarding communication about homework?

You need to know whether you are expected to monitor any kind of assignment sheet that informs the family about the student's homework.

—How and when should you report back to your supervisor regarding contact with the student's family?

• **Recognize the difference between communicating and advocating.**

Remember that communication is neutral, that it means "to make known." Advocating, on the other hand, means "to speak in favor of," or to convince someone of something. Even if at times you find yourself wanting to advocate for the family, or for the student, or for the school, DO NOT. When your job involves communicating with the student's family, you need to keep the lines of communication between the student, the family, and the school clear, open, and functioning.

This is not always easy. If there are disagreements between the various parties, it may be hard not to "take sides." Nonetheless, try to be neutral about the content of any information that is being shared, and at the same time be friendly, respectful, and non-judgmental toward everyone. Remember, it is not your job to make program or policy decisions—that is the job of your school supervisors—so advocating a particular position is overstepping your role. However, if your supervisor asks for your opinion (e.g., "What do you think we should do about his mother's request?"), do share your thoughts and ideas about what is best.

If a family member expresses concern or has a question, refer the person to your supervisor. Do not try to explain school policy or speak for another staff member, the school, or the district. In some cases, it may seem appropriate to tell the family member that you will see what you can find out. Then take the concern or question to your supervisor. Be sure to ask the supervisor who should get back to the family.

When communicating with the family, avoid jargon or initials. For example, do not use a term like IEP, BIP, or LRE unless you fully explain it or unless a family member has used the term first.

- **Make sure all your interactions with the family demonstrate that you have respect and high expectations for the student.**

Regardless of the reason for any communication, the family should perceive that you are someone who cares about the student and that you want to do everything possible to help the student achieve the identified goals. This means that you should never (even unconsciously) exhibit a defeatist attitude that suggests progress is hopeless. If you have to report to the family about any setbacks or problems, make it clear

that you are optimistic that things will get better. This is not advocating because you are not trying to convince anyone of anything. You are simply communicating optimism that the goals are achievable and that improvement is expected.

Be sure you always communicate your respect for the student. Refer to successes as evidence of what you know the student can do. Refer to problems as obstacles to be overcome on the way to achieving the goals. Never make fun of the student or use a negative name or label to describe the student. Even if a family member refers to the student as a "brat," for example, do not use a term like that. If you need to report about a really bad day in which the student was frequently rude to you, do not cover up what happened—just report what the student actually did or said without putting a label on it.

- **Be understanding and tolerant of the student's family.**

If you have frequent interactions with the student's family, you may find yourself learning more details about family members than you want to know. For example, you may learn

about aspects of their lifestyle that you do not approve of. Or you may find that you really don't like one or more family member. Furthermore, you may find yourself dealing with highly emotional situations. Just remember that your role is to communicate and that you need to keep any judgments to yourself. One thing that may help is to remind yourself that most families are doing the best they can and that (in almost ALL cases) the families do care about the students.

One last reminder: be very careful NEVER to imply that anyone caused the student's disability. Some families of children with disabilities feel tremendous guilt, and you don't want to come off as judgmental about any aspect of the family situation.

- **Be a good listener.**

Whenever you interact with the student's family, remember that communication is a two-way process. Plan to listen more than you talk. When a family member tells you something, summarize what was said. "So, you would like me to let Nan's teacher know that . . . . Is that correct?" If you are not sure what has been said, ask for clarification. "I am sorry, but could you explain that again? I want to be sure I understand what you're telling me."

- **Before having any contact with the student outside of school, be sure to get approval from your supervisor and full permission from the student's family.**

Home/School Daily Communication for: _____ **Date:** _____

SCHOOL NEWS

Morning:

Things that went well:

Something to improve:

Afternoon:

Things that went well:

Something to improve:

Something you need to know about tomorrow:

FAMILY NEWS

Please write any concerns, questions or comments you would like the school to know about or respond to.

CONTACT LOG

For: _____ Date: _____

Type of contact (phone, at school, at home, other):

Person initiating contact (family, school personnel, student):

Purpose of the Contact:

Summary of Discussion:

Things to follow-up on (who is responsible for what, by when):

CONTACT LOG

For: _____ Date: _____

Type of contact (phone, at school, at home, other):

Person initiating contact (family, school personnel, student):

Purpose of the Contact:

Summary of Discussion:

Things to follow-up on (who is responsible for what, by when):

CHAPTER 7 ACTIVITIES

THINK ABOUT IT

Use the following chart to evaluate your familiarity with the material presented in this chapter. When you have completed this activity, enter reminders about the tasks you wanted to reread or discuss into your planning calendar.

	The information was not applicable to my situation.	The information was familiar. I consistently implement the strategies presented.	The information was useful. I should reread this task at least once more this year.	Some of the information was new. I should reread this task within a month.	Much of the information was new. I should discuss it with my supervisor or with other paraeducators.
TASK 1: Understand your role as part of the team that will help the student become as independent as possible.	0	1	2	3	4
TASK 2: Get relevant background information about the student.	0	1	2	3	4
TASK 3: Be clear about what is expected of the student and what is expected of you in all situations.	0	1	2	3	4
TASK 4: Interact productively with the student.	0	1	2	3	4
TASK 5: Interact appropriately with the student's family.	0	1	2	3	4

(NOTE: On pages 205-210, in the back of the book, you will find a complete chart of all the tasks in the book. You may wish to summarize the information from each individual chapter on this single chart.)

TAKE ACTION

Implement a "Scatter Plot" system for collecting and analyzing information to help you understand a particular problem behavior exhibited by your student. The problem can be anything ranging from head-hitting to talk-outs. Use the following steps:

1. Identify the specific behavior you want to understand better or want the student to improve.

2. Define what the misbehavior looks like and sounds like. That is, describe what you see the student do and/or what you hear the student say when he or she is exhibiting the behavior. (This step will make it clear to anyone who may collect information on the behavior exactly what to look for/record.)

3. List the student's schedule, including activities and times.

4. Develop a recording code. You may use something like a slash mark, a check mark, or a shaded square to indicate that the behavior occurred. Or you may want to use different codes to indicate that different amounts of the behavior occurred. For example, you may use a "/" to indicate 1-3 occurrences of out-of-seat behavior and a "+" to indicate 4-6 occurrences of out-of-seat behavior.

5. Collect information on the behavior for at least two weeks. If you do not work with the student throughout the entire day, ask other staff members to collect the information when you are not present.

6. At the end of the two weeks, analyze the information. First, look for any patterns. Then, ask questions to develop a theory about what causes/influences the behavior.

NOTE: The "Jasmine" scenario that follows is an example of how this process works.

Jasmine Scatter Plot Example

Jasmine is a third grade student. She has a one-on-one paraeducator, Ms. Pratt, who works with her throughout the day in both the regular classroom and the resource room. In both settings, Jasmine is often disruptive—talking-out in a very loud manner. The regular classroom teacher, Mr. Eagan, feels that Jasmine talks-out all the time. Ms. Pratt, while acknowledging that Jasmine talks-out a lot, believes that there are many times when Jasmine is not talking-out. The two decide that they will collect information on the situation. Ms. Pratt records information on Jasmine's talk-outs for two weeks. (See Figure 7.6)

Figure 7.6

Scatter Plot of Jasmine Talk-Outs

Student: **Jasmine**

Date: **Week of 3/11/00 to 3/22/00**

Behavior: **Talk-outs: Any occurence in which Jasmine talks without permission**

Respondent: **Ms. Sanchez**

ACTIVITY	TIME	Day 1	Day 2	Day 3	Day 4	Day 5	Day 6	Day 7	Day 8	Day 9	Day 10
Breakfast	8:30-9:00										
Group	9:00-9:15									■	
Schedule/Assignments	9:15-9:30				■					■	
Reading	9:30-10:45										
Written Language	10:45-11:15									■	
Math	11:15-12:00	■			■		■				
Lunch	12:00-12:30				■						
Group	12:30-12:45									■	
Social Studies	12:45-1:30	■	■	■	■	■	■	■		■	■
Study Skills	1:30-2:00				■		■				
Prepare for Home	2:00-2:15				■					■	
Bus	2:20									■	

At the end of the two weeks, Mr. Eagan, Ms. Pratt, and Mrs. Sanchez (the Special Education teacher, who is Ms. Pratt's primary supervisor) meet to review the information. They first note that the highest rate of talk-outs occurred during social studies and that Thursday was the worst day of the week for the behavior. Next they note that on Day 8, Jasmine had no talk-outs at all. They realize that Jasmine's best friend, Lisa, was not at school on that particular day. They also realize that Lisa is in Jasmine's social studies class.

The team decides to move Jasmine's seat closer to Lisa's during social studies so that if Jasmine talks-out, it would not be as loud and disruptive to the rest of the class. More importantly, Mr. Eagan makes a commitment to interacting with Jasmine as soon as she enters the classroom—to catch her behaving responsibly, rather than having his interactions with her be only when she is misbehaving. Ms. Pratt will make an effort to praise Jasmine for staying on-task, raising her hand and waiting to be called on to talk, and only talking to Lisa when it is appropriate.

DISCUSS IT

Arrange with a group of colleagues to read Chapter 7 and do the Take Action activity for this chapter. Then schedule a meeting at which the group can discuss the following topics/questions.

1. Discuss some of the difficulties involved in maintaining patience and objectivity when working with the same student day after day. Brainstorm ideas for maintaining equilibrium, balance, and a sense of humor.

2. Have each person in the group identify and share an academic or behavioral problem exhibited—the student he or she works with. Remember to use objective reporting, not jargon, labels, or conclusions. After each person has shared, spend five to ten minutes, as a group, on each problem— brainstorming ideas that might help the paraeducator to help the student. If the group can't think of ideas, skim through Chapter 7 to see if any ideas from the chapter could be applicable. (REMINDER: Any changes in procedures should be cleared with a supervisor first.)

3. Have each person share any useful ideas that were gained from working through the Take Action activity.

Cumulative Chart

Use the following charts to evaluate your familiarity with the material presented in this chapter. When you have completed this activity, enter reminders about the tasks you wanted to reread or discuss into your planning calendar.

Figure 1.2 Reproducible Form

Chapter 1	The information was not applicable to my situation.	The information was familiar. I consistently implement the strategies presented.	The information was useful. I should reread this task at least once more this year.	Some of the information was new. I should reread this task within a month.	Much of the information was new. I should discuss it with my supervisor or with other paraeducators.
TASK 1: Remember the "bare essentials."	0	1	2	3	4
TASK 2: Understand the hierarchy of authority in your school	0	1	2	3	4
TASK 3: Present yourself in a professional manner	0	1	2	3	4
TASK 4: Treat everyone with dignity and respect	0	1	2	3	4
TASK 5: Be aware of some basic school-based legal issues	0	1	2	3	4

Figure 2.2 Reproducible Form

Chapter 2	The information was not applicable to my situation.	The information was familiar. I consistently implement the strategies presented.	The information was useful. I should reread this task at least once more this year.	Some of the information was new. I should reread this task within a month.	Much of the information was new. I should discuss it with my supervisor or with other paraeducators.
TASK 1: Demonstrate a positive attitude.	0	1	2	3	4
TASK 2: Use effective communication strategies.	0	1	2	3	4
TASK 3: Respect confidentiality.	0	1	2	3	4
TASK 4: Deal with disagreements productively.	0	1	2	3	4
TASK 5: Be responsible when it comes to meetings, workshops, and classes.	0	1	2	3	4

Figure 3.9 Reproducible Form

Chapter 3	The information was not applicable to my situation.	The information was familiar. I consistently implement the strategies presented.	The information was useful. I should reread this task at least once more this year.	Some of the information was new. I should reread this task within a month.	Much of the information was new. I should discuss it with my supervisor or with other paraeducators.
TASK 1: Become familiar with some basic concepts related to behavior.	0	1	2	3	4
TASK 2: Be clear about what is expected of the students and what is expected of you.	0	1	2	3	4
TASK 3: Actively monitor student behavior.	0	1	2	3	4
TASK 4: Reinforce responsible student behavior.	0	1	2	3	4
TASK 5: Respond to irresponsible student behavior in ways that will help students learn to behave more responsibly.	0	1	2	3	4
TASK 6: Understand some basic concepts related to information-based decision-making.	0	1	2	3	4
TASK 7: Prevent (and/or deal effectively with) student non-compliance.	0	1	2	3	4

Figure 4.2 Reproducible Form

Chapter 4	The information was not applicable to my situation.	The information was familiar. I consistently implement the strategies presented.	The information was useful. I should reread this task at least once more this year.	Some of the information was new. I should reread this task within a month.	Much of the information was new. I should discuss it with my supervisor or with other paraeducators.
TASK 1: Know the procedures and expectations for each common area you supervise.	0	1	2	3	4
TASK 2: Know how to effectively supervise any common area for which you have responsibility.	0	1	2	3	4
TASK 3: Be aware of specific management tips that apply to: the cafeteria, the playground, and the hallways and restrooms.	0	1	2	3	4

Figure 5.8 Reproducible Form

Chapter 5	The information was not applicable to my situation.	The information was familiar. I consistently implement the strategies presented.	The information was useful. I should reread this task at least once more this year.	Some of the information was new. I should reread this task within a month.	Much of the information was new. I should discuss it with my supervisor or with other paraeducators.
TASK 1: Know the procedures, materials, and what is expected of you.	0	1	2	3	4
TASK 2: Know the behavioral expectations for students.	0	1	2	3	4
TASK 3: Teach the behavioral expectations to students (as needed).	0	1	2	3	4
TASK 4: Use effective instructional techniques.	0	1	2	3	4
TASK 5: Manage student behavior effectively.	0	1	2	3	4

Figure 6.3 Reproducible Form

Chapter 6	The information was not applicable to my situation.	The information was familiar. I consistently implement the strategies presented.	The information was useful. I should reread this task at least once more this year.	Some of the information was new. I should reread this task within a month.	Much of the information was new. I should discuss it with my supervisor or with other paraeducators.
TASK 1: Be clear about the expectations for students and the expectations for you.	0	1	2	3	4
TASK 2: Manage independent work periods effectively.	0	1	2	3	4

Figure 7.6 Reproducible Form

Chapter 7	The information was not applicable to my situation.	The information was familiar. I consistently implement the strategies presented.	The information was useful. I should reread this task at least once more this year.	Some of the information was new. I should reread this task within a month.	Much of the information was new. I should discuss it with my supervisor or with other paraeducators.
TASK 1: Understand your role as part of the team that will help the student become as independent as possible.	0	1	2	3	4
TASK 2: Get relevant background information about the student.	0	1	2	3	4
TASK 3: Be clear about what is expected of the student and what is expected of you in all situations.	0	1	2	3	4
TASK 4: Interact productively with the student.	0	1	2	3	4
TASK 5: Interact appropriately with the student's family.	0	1	2	3	4

References

Archer, A. & Gleason, M. (1990). Skills for school success. North Billerica, MA: Curriculum Associates.

Garrity, C., Jens, K., Porter, W., Sager, N., & Short-Camilli, C. (2000). Bully-Proofing your school: A comprehensive approach for elementary schools. Longmont, CO: Sopris West.

Great Falls Public Schools (1997). Project RIDE: Responding to individual differences in education. Longmont, CO: Sopris West.

Pickett, A. L., Faison, K., & Formanek, J. (1993). A. core curriculum & training program to prepare paraeducators to work in inclusive classrooms serving school age students with disabilities. New York: The National Resource Center for Paraprofessionals in Education and Related Services, City University of New York.

Sprick, R. S. (1995). Cafeteria discipline: Positive techniques for lunchroom supervision. (Video Program). Eugene, OR: Teaching Strategies, Inc.

Sprick, R. S. (1990). Playground discipline: Positive techniques for recess supervision. (Video Program). Eugene, OR: Teaching Strategies, Inc.

Sprick, R. S., Garrison, M., and Howard, L. M. (1998). CHAMPs: A proactive and positive approach to classroom management. Longmont, CO: Sopris West.